Pacific
Passions

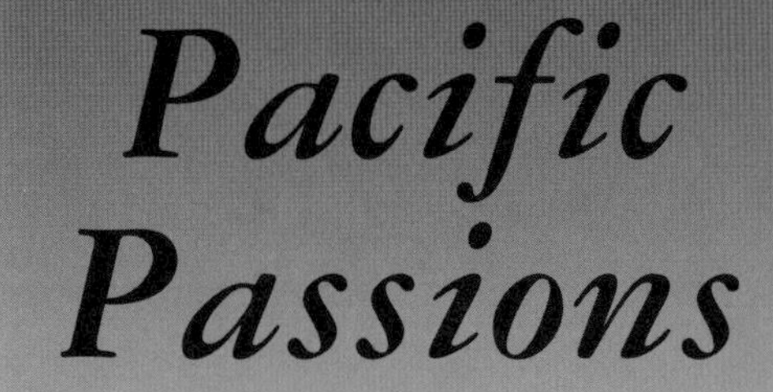

Pacific Passions

Celebrating the Flavors of the West Coast

Karen Barnaby

Whitecap Books
Vancouver/Toronto

Whitecap Books
Vancouver/Toronto

Edited by Elaine Jones
Copy-edited by Elizabeth McLean
Cover design by Designgeist
Interior design by Warren Clark
Cover illustration by Laura Cook
Typeset by Warren Clark

Printed and bound in Canada by D.W. Friesen and Sons Ltd., Altona, Manitoba.

Canadian Cataloguing in Publication Data

Barnaby, Karen
Pacific passions cookbook

Includes index
ISBN 1-55110-380-X

1. Cookery, Canadian—British Columbia style.
I. Title.
TX715.6.B37 1995   641.59711   C95-910690-1

To David Wood
and Vanipha Southalack

Contents

Appetizers, Soups and Salads

Meat

Vegetables and Grains

Introduction

I think we all have a subject we are passionate about. Mine happens to be food and cooking. All aspects of it fascinate me: history, theory, culture, chemistry and anthropology.

The foods of the Pacific Northwest have a special fascination for me. The long growing season here is especially appealing. Arugula and mache seed themselves in the fall and peek through the soil in late February. Thyme and sage stay green throughout the drizzly winter.

The greens of spring arrive—lettuces, asparagus, fiddleheads, rapini, spinach, watercress and nettles. Wildcrafters pick morel mushrooms. The first spot prawns appear in the market. Then summer bursts into a kaleidoscope of color and flavor. Salmon and halibut run, Dungeness crabs are plentiful. Fantastic fruits appear and berries are abundant. Fall brings chanterelles and pine mushrooms, squash, pumpkins, beets and Yukon Gold potatoes. In winter, oysters are at their best.

My love for seasonal eating and cooking came from my two grandmothers. For them, anything was fair game. My father's mother was French Canadian and grew up relying on the seasonal nature of food. She was a gatherer of wild foods. In spring there were fiddleheads, nettles and wild garlic, then burdock, milkweed and lamb's-quarters. After that, tiny wild strawberries, blueberries and something she called high-bush cranberries. In the fall she would make marmalade out of mountain ash berries (too bitter for my childhood taste, but I tried to eat it anyway—mountain ash sounded so romantic). She became one of the early "health-food nuts" and introduced me to odd grains and beans, carrot and beet juice, and vegetarianism.

My mother's mother was more of an urban forager. With her I ate eggplant, artichokes, avocadoes and zucchini. When berries were in season we ate berries with cream and saltines. When corn and tomatoes were around, corn and tomatoes. She baked from memory—crumb cake, cornmeal cake and seed cake with lots of caraway seeds. She made pickles and jams and jellies. I remember waking up one morning to the overpowering vinegary smell of green tomato relish. It scared me for years afterwards.

I don't mean to make this sound too idyllic. I had all the usual childhood foods too—canned vegetables, processed cheese slices (the pry-apart kind), and take-away fried chicken for birthday parties. I loved it all! It was the spirit of my grandmothers, though, that made me aware of how good seasonal eating could be. Waiting for, savoring, and saying goodbye to all the wonderful foods that come and go throughout the year is what makes them special and gives me reason to celebrate each of them as it passes through this cycle.

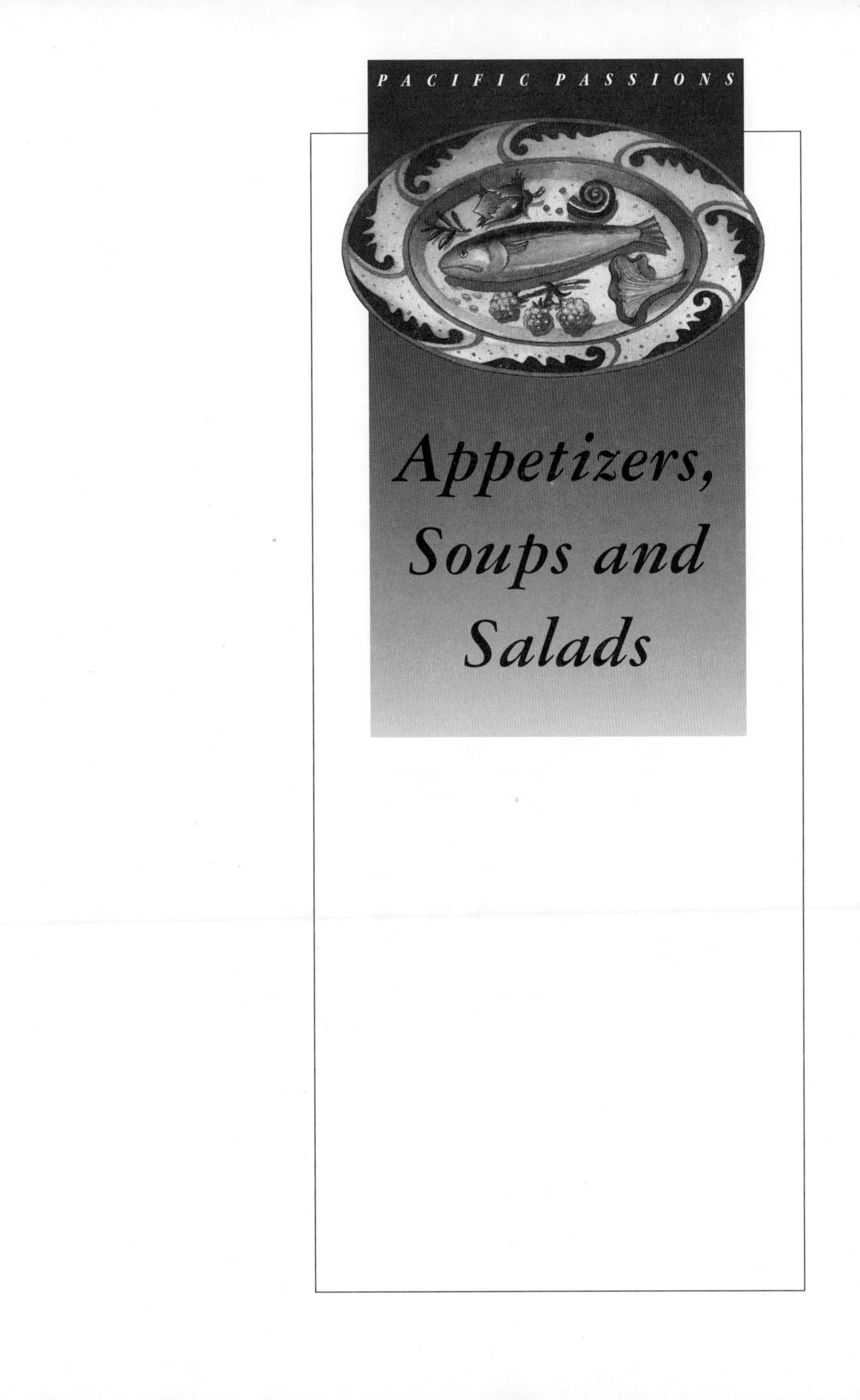
PACIFIC PASSIONS
Appetizers, Soups and Salads

Dungeness Crab and Corn Fritters

I think I have served about 100,000 of these fritters between all of the restaurants I have worked in. I like to make a sandwich with them, hot out of the pan with mayonnaise, tomatoes, lettuce and onions—a Pacific Northwest version of a Louisiana Po' Boy.

Makes 16-20 fritters

1 1/4 cups	corn kernels, fresh or thawed if frozen	310 ml
1	large egg	1
1/4 cup	finely diced onion	60 ml
3/4 cup	all-purpose flour	185 ml
1/4 cup	cornmeal	60 ml
1 tsp.	salt	5 ml
1 1/2 tsp.	sugar	7.5 ml
1 1/2 tsp.	baking powder	7.5 ml
1/2 tsp.	finely chopped fresh thyme leaves	2.5 ml
1/4 tsp.	cayenne pepper	1.2 ml
1/4 tsp.	ground black pepper	1.2 ml
3/4 lb.	Dungeness crab meat, picked over and squeezed dry	350 g
	vegetable oil for frying	

Combine the corn and egg in the work bowl of a food processor or blender. Pulse until the corn is finely chopped. Add the onion and pulse a few more times to mix well. Scrape into a bowl.

Whisk the dry ingredients together and stir into the corn mixture. Fold in the crab.

Heat 1 1/2 inches (4 cm) of oil in a large heavy frying pan. Drop in large teaspoonfuls of the batter without overcrowding the pan. Fry until they are a shade darker than golden brown. Turn and brown the other side. Keep the cooked fritters warm in a low oven while you are frying the rest. Serve with tartar sauce, cocktail sauce or Sweet and Sour Dipping Sauce, page 198.

Dungeness Crab Pancakes with Crème Fraîche and Salmon Caviar

An elegant hors d'oeuvres or first course. I sometimes serve them with a pitcher of melted butter on the side instead of the crème fraîche and caviar.

Makes 8 large or 16 small pancakes

1 cup	buttermilk	250 ml
1	large egg, separated	1
1/2 tsp.	salt	2.5 ml
4 Tbsp.	cornmeal	60 ml
3 Tbsp.	all-purpose flour	45 ml
	pinch of black pepper	
2 Tbsp.	minced green onion	30 ml
1/2 lb.	Dungeness crab meat, lightly squeezed dry	225 g
1 cup	Crème Fraîche, page 192	250 ml
4 oz.	salmon caviar	113 g

Beat the buttermilk and egg yolk together.

Sift the dry ingredients together.

Lightly whisk the wet ingredients into the dry. Fold in the green onion and crab. Beat the egg white until stiff and fold into the mixture.

Heat a heavy or nonstick frying pan over medium heat. Lightly brush the pan with oil. Use 1 or 2 tablespoons (15-30 ml) of the batter per pancake depending on the size you want. Cook until the sides of the pancake look slightly dry. Flip over and cook on the other side until lightly browned.

Top with crème fraîche and salmon caviar or bring the components to the table individually for your guests to top their own.

Peppered Oysters with Roasted Corn and Tomato Relish

Irresistible! My favorite way of eating oysters.

Serves 4-6

1 qt.	medium shucked oysters with their juice	1 L
2	bay leaves	2
2 Tbsp.	black peppercorns	30 ml
8	cloves roasted garlic, page 196, mashed to a paste	8
1/4 tsp.	ground allspice	1.2 ml
1 Tbsp.	lemon juice	15 ml

In a large frying pan, bring the oyster juice and bay leaves to a boil. Add the oysters and cook until their edges curl. Drain in a sieve that has been placed over a bowl to catch the juice.

While the oysters are draining, dry-roast the peppercorns over medium heat until they start to smell fragrant. Grind to a powder in a coffee grinder.

Return the oyster juice and bay leaves to the frying pan. Add the pepper, garlic and allspice. Bring to a boil and cook, stirring frequently, until the mixture becomes pasty. Return the oysters to the pan and coat thoroughly with the mixture. Stir in the lemon juice. Serve at room temperature or chilled with the corn and tomato relish.

Roasted Corn and Tomato Relish

1	ear fresh corn	1
4	ripe plum tomatoes, peeled, seeded and finely chopped (see Two Ways to Peel a Tomato, page 128)	4
2	thinly sliced green onions	2
2 Tbsp.	coarsely chopped cilantro leaves	30 ml
	salt and pepper	

Preheat the oven to 400°F (200°C). Cut the corn kernels from the ear. Spread them out on a baking pan and roast for 10-15 minutes, stirring occasionally, until the corn picks up a few brown spots. Remove from the oven and cool.

Combine the corn with the remaining ingredients and season with salt and pepper. Serve with the oysters.

Stir-Fried Oysters with Black Beans and Chilies

This oyster dish was named as one of the best oyster preparations in Vancouver by Jurgen Gothe. Try it and find out why. The oysters may also be served at room temperature or chilled.

If you want to double the recipe, cook it in two batches in separate pans.

Serves 3-4 as an appetizer or as part of a Chinese-style meal

1/2 pint	small, shucked oysters	250 ml
1 Tbsp.	vegetable oil	15 ml
1 1/2 tsp.	finely grated ginger	7.5 ml
2	medium cloves garlic, minced	2
1 Tbsp.	fermented black beans*	15 ml
2 Tbsp.	white wine	30 ml
3	canned plum tomatoes, drained and diced	3
1 tsp.	hot chili sauce	5 ml
2	green onions, julienned	2

*Available at Oriental markets and well-stocked supermarkets.

Drain the oysters well. Lay them out on paper towels to drain further while you are preparing the rest of the ingredients.

Heat the vegetable oil over high heat in a wok or heavy frying pan. Stir-fry the ginger until it begins to turn brown, then stir-fry the garlic until it begins to turn golden. Add the black beans. As soon as they sizzle, mix in the white wine, tomatoes and hot chili sauce. Cook until the wine evaporates, then add the oysters. Stir-fry until the oysters firm up, about 2 minutes. Toss in the green onions, stir once or twice and serve immediately on heated plates or a platter.

Spot Prawn Spring Rolls

My friend Vanipha taught me how to make spring rolls and many other Thai and Laotian dishes. Besides running her own restaurant, she also supplied spring rolls to other restaurants and caterers. Some days, she would have orders for 1,000 spring rolls. (They have to be rolled by hand—so let this be an inspiration to you.) Spring rolls are a labor of love, but just think of how impressed everyone will be. If you prefer, you can make them without the prawns.

Makes 32 spring rolls

4	cloud ear mushrooms, soaked in hot water until soft (optional)	4
3/4 cup	coarsely chopped bamboo shoots	185 ml
1/2 cup	coarsely chopped water chestnuts	125 ml
2 Tbsp.	vegetable oil	30 ml
3	medium cloves garlic, minced	3
3 cups	green cabbage, thinly sliced and chopped into fine pieces	750 ml
1 cup	grated carrot	250 ml
4	thinly sliced green onions	4
3 Tbsp.	oyster sauce*	45 ml
1/2 tsp.	black pepper	2.5 ml
3	2-oz. (50-g) packages cellophane noodles,* soaked in hot water until softened and drained	3
36	8- by 8-inch (20-cm) frozen spring roll wrappers*	36
4 Tbsp.	all-purpose flour	60 ml
2 Tbsp.	water	30 ml
16	large spot prawns or shrimp, peeled with the tail left on, and cut in half lengthwise	16
	vegetable oil for frying the spring rolls	
1 recipe	Sweet and Sour Dipping Sauce, page 198	1 recipe

*Available at Oriental markets and well-stocked supermarkets.

Remove and discard the woody stems from the cloud ear mushrooms and coarsely chop the mushrooms. In the work bowl of a food processor pulse the mushrooms, bamboo shoots and water chestnuts until everything is finely chopped. (Or finely chop by hand.) Squeeze the mixture with your hands to remove as much water as possible.

In a wok or large frying pan, heat the vegetable oil over high heat. Add the garlic and stir-fry until it turns golden. Add the cabbage and carrots. Stir-fry until the cabbage is tender-crisp. Add the green onions, oyster sauce and black pepper and stir-fry for another minute. Remove from the heat and spread out on a pan to cool.

Chop the cellophane noodles into 1-inch (2.5-cm) pieces and add to the cooled vegetable mixture. Refrigerate until cold.

Gently peel the spring roll wrappers apart and cover with a damp cloth. Stir the flour and water together to form a smooth paste. You are now ready to roll the spring rolls.

Place a wrapper on a flat surface with one of the points facing towards you. Place about 2 Tbsp. (30 ml) of the filling slightly above the middle of the wrapper. Make a neat cylinder about 4 inches (10 cm) long out of the filling. Fold the point closest to you over the filling to slightly below the point that is farthest away from you. Fold both right and left points firmly over the filling and roll once away from you. Tuck a prawn half into the right-hand side of the fold (if you are right-handed) with the tail piece protruding from the wrapper. Dab some of the flour and water paste on the top point and continue rolling up, gently but firmly, until you reach the top. Continue rolling spring rolls with the remaining filling.

In a large heavy skillet, heat 3 inches (7.5 cm) of vegetable oil to 325°F (160°C). Fry the spring rolls without over-crowding the pan until golden brown on all sides. Remove from the oil and drain on absorbent paper. Keep warm in a low oven while frying the remaining spring rolls.

Preparing Spring Rolls

Although the instructions for rolling may seem complicated at first, you will understand them completely after rolling the first spring roll. It is important that the spring rolls be tightly but gently rolled. If not, oil will seep in during the frying and make them greasy.

The filling must be moist but not wet. If there is water collecting around the filling, place it in a sieve and gently squeeze out the water. Leave the filling in the sieve while you are rolling the spring rolls. This is important because if the wrappers get wet, the spring rolls will burst during frying. Fry the spring rolls within half an hour after making them.

Vancouver Salad Rolls

Vietnamese in origin, salad rolls are light, refreshing and satisfying at the same time. You can use cooked shrimp, chicken or crab instead of salmon.

There are two approaches to making the salad rolls. You can either roll them yourself, or you can place bowls of hot water and the ingredients on large platters and instruct your guests in rolling. Perfect the rolling technique, and you will become a supreme being in their eyes.

Makes 24 rolls

2 lbs.	boneless, skinless salmon filet	900 g
1/4 cup	light soya sauce	60 ml
2 tsp.	sugar	10 ml
1 cup	light soya sauce	250 ml
1/4 cup	water	60 ml
2 Tbsp.	sugar	30 ml
1 Tbsp.	white vinegar	15 ml
1 tsp.	sesame oil	5 ml
1	2-inch (5-cm) piece of ginger, peeled and thinly sliced	1
2	green onions, thinly sliced	2
24	8-inch (20-cm) rice papers*	24
12	large leaves of leaf or butter lettuce, cut in half	12
1/4 lb.	somen noodles,* cooked and cooled	115 g
1 cup	mint leaves	250 ml
1	bunch cilantro, washed and dried	1
1/2	English cucumber, coarsely julienned	1/2
12	green onions, split in half lengthwise and cut into 2-inch (5-cm) pieces	12

*Available at Oriental markets and well-stocked supermarkets.

Preheat the broiler. Cut the salmon against the grain into 24 thin strips. Place the strips on a baking sheet that will fit under the broiler. Stir the 1/4 cup (60 ml) soya sauce and 2 tsp. (10 ml) sugar together and brush it on the salmon. Broil until the sauce sizzles and the salmon becomes opaque. Cool.

To make the dipping sauce, combine the 1 cup (250 ml) soya sauce, water, 2 Tbsp. (30 ml) sugar, vinegar, sesame oil, ginger and thinly sliced green onions in a food processor or blender and process until the ginger is puréed. Pour into small bowls for serving.

To assemble the salad rolls, have a large bowl of hot water at hand to dip the rice papers into. Arrange all the other ingredients on a large platter. Take a sheet of rice paper and inspect it for breaks. If it is broken, do not use it. Dip a rice paper into the hot water and place it on a flat surface. If you are rolling the salad rolls yourself, do as many rice papers as you have room for.

When the rice papers have become pliable, place the filling ingredients close to the bottom of the papers in this order: a piece of lettuce, a small pile of the somen noodles, a piece of the salmon, a few mint leaves, a few sprigs of cilantro, the cucumber, then the green onion.

Smear a bit of the somen noodles on the top of the rice paper. This helps the roll stick together. Fold both sides of the rice paper over the filling. Pick up the bottom edge and fold it over the filling as well. Start rolling up from the bottom, gently but firmly. Take heart, each salad roll will look better than the last. Serve immediately with the dipping sauce.

Rosemary and Rock Salt Roasted Hazelnuts

These nuts are exquisite served warm and delicious at room temperature.

Makes 2 cups (500 ml)

2 cups	hazelnuts, with skin on	500 ml
2 Tbsp.	fresh rosemary leaves	30 ml
2 tsp.	coarse salt	10 ml
1 Tbsp.	vegetable oil	15 ml

Preheat the oven to 350°F (180°C). Place the hazelnuts in a bowl and toss with the rosemary, salt and vegetable oil. Spread the nuts in a single layer on a baking sheet and roast for 10-15 minutes, stirring occasionally, until they are roasted through.

Prawn and Sweet Potato Pancakes

Serve these pancakes with Sweet and Sour Dipping Sauce, page 198. They are highly edible as the kind of leftover you eat while looking in the fridge to decide what to really eat.

Makes 16 pancakes

24	medium prawns, peeled and deveined (leave the tails on 16 of the prawns)	24
1 Tbsp.	fish sauce*	15 ml
2	cloves garlic, finely chopped	2
1/2 tsp.	ground black pepper	2.5 ml
1 cup	all-purpose flour	250 ml
1 cup	cornstarch	250 ml
1 Tbsp.	sugar	15 ml
1 tsp.	salt	5 ml
1 tsp.	baking powder	5 ml
3/4 tsp.	turmeric	4 ml
1 1/4 cups	cold water	310 ml
1/2 lb.	sweet potatoes, peeled and julienned	225 g
2	green onions, thinly sliced	2
	vegetable oil for frying	

*Available at Oriental markets and well-stocked supermarkets.

Combine the 16 tail-on prawns with the fish sauce, garlic and pepper. Cover and refrigerate. Finely chop the remaining prawns and set aside.

In a large bowl, combine the flour, cornstarch, sugar, salt, baking powder and turmeric. Slowly whisk in the cold water until the batter is smooth. Add the chopped prawns, sweet potato and green onions. Mix well.

In a large heavy frying pan, heat 1 1/2 inches (4 cm) of oil over medium high heat. Oil the backs of 2 large baking sheets and place 8 mounds of the batter on each. Flatten the mounds and press a prawn on to each of the cakes. Slide a few cakes into the oil and fry until golden brown on the bottom. Flip over and fry on the other side until golden brown. Remove from the pan and drain. The pancakes may be kept warm in a low oven while you are frying the rest. Serve immediately.

Fish Sauce

This is a salty condiment used to season food in Southeast Asian cooking, the same way salt or soya sauce is used. As a general rule, the lighter and more golden-hued the sauce looks in the bottle the better its quality.

Salmon Cooked on a Plate with Tomato Basil Relish

To make this you need four heat-proof plates—the modern-day equivalent of cooking food on hot slabs of rock. The salmon makes a very satisfying sizzle when it hits the plates.

Be careful to put the plates on a heat-proof surface. Once, during a cooking demonstration of this dish, I welded a plate to a plastic cutting board!

Serves 4

4	medium, ripe tomatoes, seeded and finely diced	4
1 tsp.	salt	5 ml
2 Tbsp.	thinly sliced green onions	30 ml
2 Tbsp.	thinly sliced basil leaves	30 ml
1 Tbsp.	olive oil	15 ml
	salt and pepper to taste	
4	2-oz. (60-g) pieces of salmon filet, thinly sliced on the diagonal to 1/4-inch (.6-cm) thickness	4
	vegetable oil	

Combine the diced tomatoes and salt. Place in a strainer and allow to drain for 1/2 hour. Place the drained tomatoes in a bowl and stir in the onions, basil and olive oil. Season with salt and pepper.

Preheat the oven to 500°F (260°C). Place 4 heat-proof plates in the oven in a single layer for 20 minutes. While the plates are heating, brush the salmon lightly with vegetable oil and season with salt and pepper.

Remove the plates from the oven and immediately place a piece of salmon on each plate. Let the salmon cook for a minute, then spoon the tomato relish on top. Serve immediately, warning your guests that the plates are hot.

Honey Pickled Salmon

For an interesting contrast of texture and temperature, serve this salmon with hot, boiled new potatoes.

Serves 8-10 as an appetizer

2 1/2 lbs.	boneless, skinless salmon cut into 1-inch (2.5-cm) chunks	1 kg
2 tsp.	salt	10 ml
1	small onion, peeled and cut into 1-inch (2.5-cm) rings	1

Pickling Mixture

1 cup	cider vinegar	250 ml
1 cup	water	250 ml
1/2 cup	fragrant honey	125 ml
1	bay leaf crumbled	1
1/2 tsp.	yellow mustard seeds	2.5 ml
1/2 tsp.	black mustard seeds	2.5 ml
1 tsp.	whole cloves	5 ml
1 tsp.	whole black peppercorns	5 ml
1 tsp.	whole white peppercorns	5 ml
1 tsp.	coriander seeds	5 ml

Toss the salmon cubes with the salt and let sit for 1/2 hour. Rinse and pat dry. Layer in a large bowl with the onion rings.

Combine the pickling mixture in a noncorrodible saucepan. Bring to a boil, reduce the heat to low, and simmer partially covered for 45 minutes. Pour the hot pickling mixture over the salmon. Insert a knife or chopstick into the salmon and jiggle it to release trapped air bubbles. Cool to room temperature and refrigerate for at least 24 hours before serving. Keeps for 1 week.

To serve, drain the salmon from the pickling liquid and serve as is or mix with 1 cup (250 ml) sour cream or crème fraîche (page 192), 1 Tbsp. (15 ml) coarsely chopped dill and 1 Tbsp. (15 ml) finely minced green onion.

Lamb Tartare

I know this recipe may seem a bit odd, but it is truly delicious. If you are a fan of steak tartare or carpaccio, add this to your repertoire.

Serves 6-8

1 lb.	very fresh, lean lamb that has been trimmed of fat and sinews (loin or leg is a good choice)	450 g
1 cup	fine bulgur	250 ml
1 cup	finely diced onion	250 ml
1/4 tsp.	cinnamon	1.2 ml
1/8 tsp.	allspice	.5 ml
2 tsp.	ground cumin	10 ml
1-2 tsp.	salt	5-10 ml
1/2 tsp.	ground black pepper	2.5 ml
	cucumber slices, radishes and onion wedges for garnish	

Cut the lamb into 1/2-inch (1-cm) cubes. Lay flat on a plate without overlapping and place in the freezer until half frozen.

Place the bulgur in a sieve and rinse under cold water. Let drain.

When the lamb is almost frozen, place all the ingredients except garnishes in a food processor and pulse until the lamb has just turned into a paste. Check for seasoning and add more salt if necessary. Cover and refrigerate until ready to serve.

To serve, spread the tartare onto a plate, making a nice even mound. Score with the back of a knife in a diamond pattern. Garnish with the vegetables (use them to scoop up the tartare) and serve with slices of good bread or crackers.

Chinatown Pâté with Fermented Black Beans

This pâté has an intriguing, earthy flavor that comes from the fermented black beans. Serve it thinly sliced with good bread or melba toast, hot Chinese mustard, pickled ginger, and hoisin sauce.

Makes 1 loaf, about 2 pounds (900 g)

2 Tbsp.	vegetable oil	30 ml
2 Tbsp.	finely chopped garlic	30 ml
1/2 cup	fermented black beans*, rinsed and drained	125 ml
1 1/2 lbs.	pork shoulder, finely ground	675 g
1 lb.	salt pork, finely ground	450 g
1/2 cup	white wine	125 ml
3	large eggs	3
1 Tbsp.	Szechuan peppercorns, coarsely ground	15 ml
1 tsp.	black pepper	5 ml

*Available at Oriental markets and well-stocked supermarkets.

Heat the oil in a small frying pan over high heat and fry the garlic until it sizzles. Add the black beans and when they sizzle, remove from the heat.

Combine all the ingredients, including the garlic and black beans, in a large bowl. Beat well until everything is thoroughly mixed. Cover and refrigerate overnight.

Preheat the oven to 350°F (180°C). Pack the pâté mixture into an 8- by 5-inch (20- by 12.5-cm) loaf pan. Cover securely with tin foil and place in a larger, deeper pan. Pour hot water into the larger pan so that it comes 2 inches (5 cm) up the sides of the loaf pan. Place in the oven and bake for 1 hour and 40 minutes, or until a thermometer inserted in the middle of the loaf reads 165°F (75°C).

Remove from the oven and let the pâté cool completely in the water bath. Weight the pâté down and refrigerate for at least 2 days before serving.

Garden Antipasto

This antipasto is great on a sandwich, as a sauce for grilled meats, as part of an antipasto plate, or as a dip for bread or corn chips. Try it as a dip alongside the smoked eggplant purée, page16. They're made for each other.

Serves 4-6

1 1/2 lbs.	ripe plum tomatoes, peeled, seeded and coarsely chopped or 1 28-oz. (796-ml) can plum tomatoes, well drained and coarsely chopped (see Two Ways to Peel a Tomato, page 128)	675 g
2	hot pickled cherry tomatoes, stemmed and chopped	2
1/2	coarsely chopped green pepper	1/2
1 cup	coarsely chopped carrots	250 ml
6	radishes, trimmed and cut in half	6
1 cup	coarsely chopped onions	250 ml
1/2 cup	coarsely chopped celery	125 ml
3	cloves garlic, chopped	3
1/4 cup	olive oil	60 ml
1 tsp.	ground cumin	5 ml
	salt to taste	

Combine all ingredients except the salt in a medium-sized heavy pot. Bring to a boil, then reduce the heat to medium and cook, stirring frequently, for 15 minutes, until the liquid has almost evaporated. Season with salt. Remove from the pot and spread onto a plate to cool.

When the mixture is cool, place in a food processor or blender and pulse until the mixture is finely chopped but not puréed. Keeps for 1 week, covered and refrigerated.

Smoked Eggplant Purée

This is one of my favorite starters for a casual hot-weather dinner. Serve it with a good bread, cucumbers, tomatoes, radishes and green onions for dipping. It also makes an excellent spread on a tomato or cucumber sandwich.

Make sure that the eggplant is charred in several places, as this is where it gets its smoky flavor.

Serves 4-6

2	medium eggplants, about 1 3/4-2 lbs. (800-900 g)	2
1	medium clove garlic, minced	1
1 tsp.	salt	5 ml
1 cup	sour cream or yogurt	250 ml
1 Tbsp.	lemon juice	15 ml

Preheat the barbecue or broiler on high. Prick the eggplant in several places with a fork. Place on the barbecue or 6 inches (15 cm) from the broiler and grill, turning to grill all sides until the eggplant is completely soft, collapsed, and charred in a few places. Remove from the heat and open the eggplant on one side. Place open side down in a strainer and let the eggplant drain for 30 minutes to 1 hour, until it has cooled completely.

When the eggplant is cooled and has finished draining, scrape the pulp from the skin. Keep all the brownish bits of eggplant that are close to the skin, as they give the purée its smoky flavor. Mash the garlic to a paste with the salt. Combine the eggplant, garlic, sour cream or yogurt and lemon juice in the work bowl of a food processor or blender and purée until smooth, or combine with a fork if you like a chunky texture. Transfer to a bowl. Cover and refrigerate until serving time. The purée keeps 3-4 days, covered and refrigerated.

Grilled Asparagus with Sesame Mayonnaise

Asparagus is so versatile—it can be eaten hot or cold, grilled, steamed or stir-fried, and it adapts to diverse seasonings. I like to cook asparagus a bit more than "al dente." Its true flavor and succulence emerge then.

For a change of flavor and a splash of color, serve the grilled asparagus with Beet Vinaigrette, page 38.

Toasting Sesame Seeds

Heat a heavy frying pan over medium-low heat. Roast the sesame seeds until they are lightly toasted, stirring constantly and tasting occasionally. Spread on a plate to cool.

Serves 4-6

1 1/2 lbs.	fresh, medium-sized asparagus, trimmed	675 g
1 tsp.	vegetable oil	5 ml
	salt and pepper to taste	
1 cup	mayonnaise	250 ml
1 Tbsp.	sesame oil	15 ml
1-2 tsp.	lemon juice, to taste	5-10 ml
1 tsp.	white sesame seeds, toasted	5 ml
1 tsp.	black sesame seeds, toasted	5 ml

Bring a large pot of water to a boil. Salt generously and add the asparagus. Cook for 1-2 minutes until the asparagus turns bright green. Drain. Cool under cold running water. Drain and pat dry.

Toss with the vegetable oil and a pinch of salt and pepper. Set aside until ready to grill.

Mix the mayonnaise, sesame oil and lemon juice together. Cover and refrigerate until ready to serve.

Preheat the barbecue to high. Grill the asparagus until lightly marked.

You can serve the asparagus hot or cold. If serving it hot, place on serving plates immediately and serve with the mayonnaise on the side. Garnish with the sesame seeds. If you are serving it cold, spread the asparagus on a plate and cool to room temperature, then serve as above.

Frittered Asparagus

Similar to tempura but less fussy, this batter can be used with many vegetables. Sweet potato is a personal favorite. Serve this with the sesame mayonnaise from the Grilled Asparagus on page 17 or with lemon wedges.

Serves 4-6

1/2 cup	chickpea flour*	125 ml
1/2 cup	rice flour*	125 ml
1/4 tsp.	baking soda	1.2 ml
3/4 tsp.	salt	4 ml
1/2 tsp.	pepper	2.5 ml
1 cup	water	250 ml
1 1/2 Tbsp.	poppy seeds	20 ml
2 tsp.	crushed coriander seeds	10 ml
	vegetable oil for frying	
1 1/2 lbs.	asparagus, trimmed	675 g

*Available at East Indian markets and well-stocked supermarkets.

Combine the chickpea flour, rice flour, baking soda, salt and pepper. Whisk in the water. Mix in the poppy seeds and crushed coriander seeds just before you are going to use the batter.

Fill a large, deep pot or frying pan with oil to a depth of 2 inches (5 cm). Heat over medium heat to 350°F (180°C). Give the batter a quick stir. Dip the asparagus into the batter, making sure it is evenly coated. It will thinly coat the asparagus. Without overcrowding, fry the asparagus for 4-5 minutes, stirring occasionally until it is reddish brown.

Drain on several layers of paper towels and keep warm in a low oven while frying the remainder of the asparagus. Let the oil come back up to temperature before frying another batch. Serve immediately.

Dungeness Crab and Black Bean Soup

I love the contrast of the spicy soup with the sweet shreds of crab. It is the sort of flavor that I wish could go on forever.

Serves 6-8

1 cup	dried black beans	250 ml
2 Tbsp.	vegetable oil	30 ml
1 cup	diced onion	250 ml
2	cloves garlic, minced	2
1/2 cup	diced celery	125 ml
1/2 cup	carrots, peeled and diced	125 ml
1/2 cup	diced red pepper	125 ml
1 1/2 tsp.	ground cumin	7.5 ml
1 tsp.	ground coriander	5 ml
1/2 tsp.	dried oregano	2.5 ml
1/8 tsp.	cayenne pepper	.6 ml
1/2	28-oz. (796-ml) can plum tomatoes, drained	1/2
	salt and pepper to taste	
1/2 lb.	Dungeness crab meat, picked over	225 g
1/2 cup	sour cream or yogurt	125 ml
2 Tbsp.	chopped cilantro	30 ml

Place the beans in a large saucepan, and cover them with 4 quarts (4 L) of cold water. Bring to a boil, then turn the heat down to a simmer and skim off any foam that rises to the top. Simmer, replenishing the water as necessary, until the beans are tender, anywhere from 2-3 hours depending on the age of the beans. Drain the beans, reserving 10 cups (2.5 L) of the cooking liquid.

Heat the vegetable oil in a large saucepan over medium heat. Add the onion, garlic, celery, carrots, and pepper. Sauté until the vegetables are soft but not browned. Add the cumin, coriander, oregano, cayenne pepper, tomatoes, beans and cooking liquid. Bring to a boil, then reduce the heat to a simmer. Simmer for 1/2 hour. Add salt and pepper.

Remove from the heat and cool slightly. Reserve 1/2 cup (125 ml) of the bean mixture and purée the rest in a food mill, food processor or blender. Return to the pot, add the reserved beans and reheat to a simmer, thinning with a bit of water if the soup seems too thick. Stir in the crab meat and ladle into bowls. Garnish with the sour cream or yogurt and cilantro.

Clam Chowder

What makes this chowder really good are the sweet and tender Manila clams that grow so plentifully in this area. I prefer not to put bacon in chowder. Instead, I like to use a local delicacy called Indian Candy. Indian Candy is made from sugar-cured salmon bellies that are cut into strips and smoked until they are almost dry. If it is available in your area, add a small handful, finely chopped, when you are sautéeing the onions and celery.

Serves 6

4 lbs.	fresh clams, in their shells	1.8 kg
4 Tbsp.	unsalted butter	60 ml
1/2 cup	diced onion	125 ml
1/2 cup	diced celery	125 ml
4 Tbsp.	all-purpose flour	60 ml
2 cups	clam nectar, heated	500 ml
	salt and pepper to taste	
2 cups	peeled diced potatoes, cooked until tender and drained	500 ml
1 cup	whipping cream	250 ml

Scrub the clams and place in a large pot. Steam over high heat, shaking the pot occasionally, until the clams open. Drain the clams, reserving the juice. Strain the juice. Remove the clams from the shells and chop coarsely.

Melt the butter over low heat in a large heavy pot. Sauté the onion and celery until they are translucent. Add the flour and stir for a few minutes. Slowly whisk in the heated clam nectar and the reserved liquid from the drained clams, ensuring that there are no lumps. Bring to a boil then reduce to a simmer. Cook for 20 minutes. Season with salt and pepper.

When ready to serve, add the potatoes and heat through. Add the cream and the reserved chopped clams. Heat through and serve.

Corn, Fennel and Salmon Chowder

Serve this chowder with Soda Bread, page 178.

Serves 6-8

4 Tbsp.	unsalted butter	60 ml
1	fennel bulb, trimmed and diced (save some of the feathery green fronds for garnish)	1
2 cups	peeled and diced onion	500 ml
1 cup	diced celery	250 ml
2 cups	corn kernels, fresh or thawed if frozen	500 ml
6 cups	milk	1.5 L
2 cups	half-and-half cream	500 ml
2 lbs.	skinless, boneless salmon, cut into 1-inch (2.5-cm) cubes	900 g
2 cups	diced potatoes, cooked until tender and drained	500 ml
	salt and pepper to taste	

Melt the butter in a large saucepan over medium heat. Sauté the fennel, onions and celery until the vegetables are soft but not browned. Add the corn, milk and cream and bring to a simmer. Cook, stirring frequently, until the corn is tender, about 10 minutes.

Add the salmon and potatoes and season with salt and pepper. Simmer until the salmon is cooked, about 10 minutes longer. Serve immediately, garnished with the fennel fronds.

Vegetable and White Bean Soup with Walnut and Cilantro Pesto

A warming soup to break the monotony of those seemingly endless wet winter days. Pass the bowl of pesto for your guests to add to their soup as they please.

Serves 6-8

1 lb.	dried white navy beans	450 g
2 Tbsp.	olive oil	30 ml
2 cups	diced onions	500 ml
1 cup	each diced celery, carrots and turnip	250 ml
3 cups	chopped green cabbage	750 ml
2	bay leaves	2
12 cups	chicken stock or water	3 L
1/2 lb.	sliced green beans	225 g
2 cups	diced zucchini	500 ml
2 cups	chopped spinach	500 ml
	salt and pepper to taste	

Place the navy beans in a large pot and cover with at least 6 inches (15 cm) of water. Bring to a boil, then turn the heat down to a lively simmer. Skim off any foam that rises to the top. Simmer until the beans are very tender, about 1 1/2 hours, adding water as needed. Drain the beans.

In a large heavy pot, heat the olive oil over medium heat. Add the onions, celery and carrots and sauté until translucent. Add the turnip, cabbage, bay leaves and stock or water. Bring to a boil, then turn down to a simmer. Season lightly with salt and cook for 1 hour. Add the remaining vegetables and white beans. Cook for half an hour longer. The soup will be rather thick. Thin with stock or water if you wish. Adjust the seasoning to taste.

Walnut and Cilantro Pesto

1 1/2	bunches cilantro, coarse stems cut off	1 1/2
4	cloves garlic, coarsely chopped	4
1/2 cup	shelled walnut halves	125 ml
	salt and pepper to taste	
1/2 cup	extra virgin olive oil	125 ml

Place the cilantro, garlic, walnuts and salt and pepper in the work bowl of a food processor or blender. With the motor running, pour in the olive oil in a smooth steady stream. Pulse on and off until a coarse paste is formed. Transfer to a bowl and cover until ready to serve.

Yellow Split Pea Gazpacho

This soup is a bit more "meaty" than traditional gazpacho but every bit as refreshing. Don't serve it too cold; the split peas tend to turn into jelly. If you want to dress up this soup, add a small handful of cooked shrimp or Dungeness crab meat to each serving.

Serves 4-6

1 cup	yellow split peas	250 ml
8 cups	water	2 L
1/2 tsp.	turmeric	2.5 ml
	salt and pepper	
	cayenne pepper to taste	
1/2 tsp.	ground cumin seeds	2.5 ml
2	large, tomatoes, peeled and diced (see Two Ways to Peel a Tomato, page 128)	2
1/2	English cucumber, diced	1/2
2	green onions, thinly sliced	2
2 Tbsp.	coarsely chopped cilantro	30 ml
	lemon juice to taste	
1 cup	yogurt (optional)	250 ml

Place the split peas and water in a large pot and bring to a boil. Skim off any foam that rises to the top, turn down to a simmer and add the turmeric. Cook until the split peas have disintegrated, about 1 1/2 hours. Remove from the heat and season with the salt, pepper, cayenne and cumin. Measure and add enough water to make 8 cups (2 L). Whisk vigorously to a smooth texture and let cool completely. (The split peas may be prepared up to 3 days in advance. Cover and refrigerate. Bring to room temperature and whisk until smooth before continuing.)

Add the tomatoes, cucumber, onions and cilantro. Taste and adjust the seasoning, adding lemon juice to tweak the flavor. Chill for half an hour and serve with a dollop of yogurt if you like.

Winter Bread Soup

The inspiration for this soup came from Christopher at Ecco Il Pane, one of Vancouver's best traditional Italian bakeries. Most cities, large and small, now have bakeries which make traditional Italian breads. It is well worth seeking out their soulful breads.

This soup feeds a crowd and is better the day after it is made. If you are making this in Vancouver, be sure to make it and eat it with one of Christopher's wonderful breads.

Parmesan Rinds

By grating your own Parmesan or grana padano, you will have the added bonus of the rinds. When you can grate no more cheese from the rinds, freeze them and use them later in soups, stews and tomato sauces. They will provide a savory flavor, aroma and succulence. Grana padano is made by the Parmesan method in areas outside of Parma. It is less expensive than true Parmesan, and some large supermarkets sell it in wedges as Parmesan cheese.

Makes 24 cups (6 L)

1 cup	dried navy beans	250 ml
3 Tbsp.	olive oil	45 ml
1 cup	peeled and diced carrots	250 ml
1 cup	diced onions	250 ml
1 cup	diced celery	250 ml
1 Tbsp.	finely chopped parsley	15 ml
4	cloves garlic, finely minced	4
16 cups	chicken stock or water	4 L
1	28-oz. (796-ml) can plum tomatoes with juice, finely chopped	1
1 cup	each peeled and diced parsnips and turnips	250 ml
2 cups	peeled and diced sweet potatoes	500 ml
2 cups	finely chopped green or savoy cabbage	500 ml
1	bunch green kale, stem and central rib removed, finely chopped	1
2	large Parmesan or grana padano rinds (optional)	2
1	bay leaf	1
6 cups	stale, good-quality bread, crusts removed and diced	1.5 L
	salt and pepper to taste	

Place the navy beans in a large pot, cover with cold water and bring to a boil. Cook for 1-2 hours, replenishing the water as necessary until the beans are tender. Drain and set aside.

In a very large pot, heat the olive oil over medium heat. Sauté the carrots, onion, celery, parsley and garlic until lightly browned. Add the chicken stock or water and the tomatoes. Bring to a boil and add the remaining vegetables, cheese rinds, bay leaf and the cooked navy beans. Season lightly with salt and simmer for 1/2 hour.

Add the bread and cook for 1 hour longer, or until the bread has dissolved. Season with the salt and pepper. This is a rather thick soup. Add more stock or water if you like it a bit thinner.

Red Bean, Tomato and Summer Squash Soup with Parsley Pesto

I like to serve this soup barely chilled on sultry summer nights. Pass the parsley pesto separately to add to each serving.

Serves 6

3 Tbsp.	olive oil	45 ml
1	large onion, finely diced	1
2	cloves garlic, minced	2
2 Tbsp.	fresh oregano leaves or 1 tsp. (5 ml) dried	30 ml
2 Tbsp.	fresh thyme leaves or 1 tsp. (5 ml) dried	30 ml
6	large ripe tomatoes, diced	6
6 cups	chicken stock	1.5 L
3 cups	cooked red kidney beans	750 ml
	salt and pepper to taste	
1	medium yellow zucchini, thinly sliced into half-moons	1
1	medium green zucchini, thinly sliced into half-moons	1
1/2 cup	small shell-shaped pasta	125 ml

In a large saucepan, heat the olive oil over low heat. Cook the onion, garlic, oregano and thyme until the onion is soft but not brown. Add the tomatoes, chicken stock, and beans. Bring to a boil, then reduce to a simmer. Simmer for 20-30 minutes until the tomatoes have fallen apart. Season with salt and pepper. Add the zucchini and pasta to the soup and simmer for 15 minutes longer. While the soup is cooking, make the pesto.

Parsley Pesto

2 cups	fresh parsley leaves, packed	500 ml
1	clove garlic, minced	1
1/4 cup	olive oil	60 ml
3 Tbsp.	Parmesan cheese	45 ml
1/2 tsp.	salt	2.5 ml

Combine the pesto ingredients in the work bowl of a food processor or blender. Pulse until the parsley is finely chopped.

Potato, Kale and Oyster Soup

The inspiration for this soup came from the Portuguese soup called Caldo Verde, which uses smoked Portuguese chourico sausage instead of the oysters. I think this version is almost as good as the original.

Serves 6-8

4 Tbsp.	vegetable oil	60 ml
3	medium onions, thinly sliced	3
2 lbs.	potatoes, peeled and thinly sliced (russets or Yukon Golds are a good choice)	900 g
10 cups	chicken stock or water	2.5 L
1 tsp.	salt	5 ml
1 lb.	kale, stems removed and washed	450 g
1 qt.	oysters, cut into four pieces if large	1 L
	ground black pepper to taste	

Heat the oil in a large pot, and sauté the onions until soft but not browned. Add the potatoes, chicken stock or water and salt. Bring to a boil. Turn the heat down to a simmer and cook until the potatoes are very tender, about 1 hour.

Purée the soup in a food processor, blender or food mill and return to the pot (see Puréeing, page 195). Bring to a simmer. Thinly shred the kale—the thinner, the better. Add to the soup and simmer for 20 minutes.

Just before serving add the oysters to the simmering soup and stir for a few minutes. Season with the black pepper (I like to use a lot!). Serve immediately.

Potato Soup with Horseradish and Caraway

If you like punchy flavors, serve this soup with a salad tossed with crumbled blue cheese and a loaf of bread.

Serves 4-6

4 Tbsp.	unsalted butter	60 ml
3	medium onions, thinly sliced	3
2 lbs.	Yukon Gold or russet potatoes, peeled and thinly sliced	900 g
10 cups	water or chicken stock	2.5 L
	pinch of salt	
2 Tbsp.	prepared horseradish	30 ml
2 tsp.	caraway seeds	10 ml
	salt and pepper to taste	
1/2 cup	18% cream (optional)	125 ml

Heat the butter in a large pot and sauté the onions over medium-low heat until very soft but not browned. Add the potatoes, water or stock and a bit of salt. Bring to a boil, then turn the heat to low and simmer until the potatoes are very soft, 30-40 minutes.

Remove the soup from the heat and purée in a food processor, blender or food mill until smooth. Add the horseradish, caraway seeds and salt and pepper. (The soup can be made up to 2 days in advance. Cool, cover and refrigerate until ready to use.)

When ready to serve, reheat gently to the boiling point. If desired, stir in the cream before serving.

Potato, Stinging Nettle and Lovage Soup

Nettles are one of the first greens of spring and are rumored to have blood-cleansing properties. Besides using them as a vegetable, I like to add them to soups and sauces. (Be sure to wear rubber gloves when handling them.) Lovage is a celery-flavored perennial herb. If you cannot find it or do not grow it, substitute the inner heart and leaves of one head of celery.

Serves 4-6

2	medium potatoes, peeled and diced	2
2	medium onions, thinly sliced	2
6 cups	chicken stock or water	1.5 L
	pinch of salt	
1/2 lb.	nettle leaves	225 g
1/2 cup	lovage leaves, loosely packed	125 ml
	salt and pepper to taste	
	sour cream, Crème Fraîche (page 192) or yogurt for garnishing	

Combine the potatoes, onions and chicken stock in a large pot. Add a bit of salt and bring to a boil. Add the nettle and lovage leaves. Turn down to a simmer and cook until the potatoes are tender, 30-40 minutes.

Remove from the heat and purée in a food processor, food mill or blender (see Puréeing, page 195). Taste and adjust the seasoning with salt and pepper. Reheat and ladle into soup bowls. Swirl in the sour cream, crème fraîche or yogurt just before serving.

Curried Carrot and Turnip Soup

Although we tend to think of root vegetables in the winter, we should remember them in late summer when they are fresh and sweet. This soup is delicious served chilled in the summer.

Serves 6

6 cups	chicken stock	1.5 L
3	medium carrots, peeled and chopped	3
3	small turnips, peeled and chopped	3
	salt to taste	
3 Tbsp.	unsalted butter	45 ml
1	large onion, finely diced	1
2 tsp.	curry powder	10 ml
2 Tbsp.	flour	30 ml
1 Tbsp.	brown sugar	15 ml
	salt and pepper to taste	
1 cup	sour cream or yogurt	250 ml
2 Tbsp.	chopped cilantro	30 ml

Combine the chicken stock, carrots and turnips in a large saucepan. Bring to a boil and season lightly with salt. Reduce the heat to medium and simmer until the vegetables are very tender, 30-45 minutes. Remove from the heat and cool slightly. Purée in a food processor, blender or food mill (see Puréeing, page 195).

Melt the butter over low heat in a large saucepan and cook the onion until soft. Add the curry powder and flour and stir for a few minutes. Add the brown sugar and slowly whisk in the puréed soup. Bring to a boil and season to taste. Remove from the heat and whisk in the sour cream or yogurt. Pour into bowls and sprinkle the cilantro on top.

Arugula Salad with Grilled Prawns and Lemon Tarragon Dressing

You may use peeled prawns if you prefer, but I find grilling the prawns with the shell on makes them more succulent and enjoyable to eat.

Serves 4

1	large bunch arugula	1
12	large, head-on prawns	12
	salt and pepper	
4	1-inch-thick (2.5-cm) slices of sturdy bread	4
1	clove garlic, peeled	1

Stem, wash and dry the arugula. Place in a plastic bag and refrigerate.

Trim the legs and feelers from the prawns with a pair of scissors.

Preheat the barbecue or broiler to medium high. Lightly salt and pepper the prawns and grill or broil 2-3 minutes on each side. Remove from the grill. Grill the bread on both sides and rub the most attractive side with the clove of garlic.

Place a piece of bread on each plate. Arrange the arugula and three of the prawns on top of the bread. Drizzle Lemon Tarragon Dressing over all and serve immediately.

Lemon Tarragon Dressing

1 Tbsp.	lemon juice	15 ml
1 Tbsp.	finely chopped fresh tarragon	15 ml
1/4 tsp.	salt	1.2 ml
1/4 tsp.	crushed black pepper	1.2 ml
5 Tbsp.	extra virgin olive oil	75 ml

Whisk the lemon juice, tarragon, salt and pepper together. Slowly beat in the olive oil. Refrigerate until ready to use.

Spinach and Smoked Salmon with Sweet and Sour Cream Dressing

For an easy meal, start with Potato Soup with Horseradish and Caraway, page 26, and move on to this salad, served with light rye or sourdough bread.

Serves 4

1	large bunch spinach, approx. 12 oz. (350 g), stemmed, washed and dried	1
3 oz.	sliced smoked salmon, cut into thin strips	85 g
3 Tbsp.	cider vinegar	45 ml
2 tsp.	sugar	10 ml
1/2 tsp.	salt	2.5 ml
1/2 cup	whipping cream	125 ml
2 Tbsp.	vegetable oil	30 ml
3/4 cup	red onion, sliced into thin half moons, loosely packed	185 ml

Place the spinach and smoked salmon in a large bowl. Combine the vinegar, sugar, salt and cream.

In a noncorrodible pan, heat the vegetable oil over medium heat. Add the onions and stir to coat the onions with the oil. Add the cream mixture and bring to a boil. Reduce until the dressing thickens slightly. Remove from the heat and pour immediately over the spinach and smoked salmon. Toss well and serve on warm plates.

Red Lettuce with Roasted Peppers, Feta and Marjoram Vinaigrette

This salad is a great combination of colors and tastes. It is especially good with pork and chicken.

Serves 6

1	head red leaf lettuce	1
1	small head radicchio	1
2 Tbsp.	red wine vinegar	30 ml
2 Tbsp.	finely chopped shallots	30 ml
1/2 tsp.	salt	2.5 ml
2 tsp.	honey	10 ml
2 tsp.	finely chopped fresh marjoram, or 3/4 tsp. (4 ml) dried marjoram	10 ml
2/3 cup	extra virgin olive oil	160 ml
1/2 tsp.	freshly ground black pepper	2.5 ml
3	red peppers, roasted, peeled and cut into 1-inch (2.5-cm) strips (see Roasting Peppers, page 70)	3
1/2 lb.	feta cheese, crumbled	225 g

Wash and dry the lettuce. Core and separate the radicchio leaves. Arrange on a platter or individual plates. Cover with a damp cloth and refrigerate until serving time.

Whisk the vinegar, shallots, salt, honey and marjoram together. Slowly beat in the olive oil and pepper.

To serve, scatter the peppers and feta over the salad. Whisk the dressing to recombine the ingredients and drizzle over the salad. Serve immediately.

Fusilli with Buttermilk, Tomato and Basil Dressing

This pasta salad creates a fan club whenever it is served. Let it sit overnight for the flavors to blend.

Serves 8

5	large, ripe tomatoes, chopped	5
1 cup	prepared mayonnaise	250 ml
1 tsp.	salt	5 ml
1/4 tsp.	pepper	1.2 ml
2	cloves garlic, minced	2
1 1/4 cups	buttermilk	310 ml
1 cup	fresh basil leaves	250 ml
1 lb.	dried fusilli or rotini	450 g
1	large tomato cut into 1/2-inch (1-cm) cubes	1

In a food processor or blender combine the tomatoes, mayonnaise, salt, pepper, garlic and buttermilk. Process until finely puréed. Add the basil and pulse a few times until chopped. (If making it by hand, chop the tomatoes to a pulp and whisk with the mayonnaise, salt, pepper, garlic and buttermilk until smooth. Chop the basil and stir into the dressing.)

Cook the fusilli or rotini in a large pot of salted boiling water until barely tender. Drain and cool under cold water. Drain well and place in a bowl. Add the dressing and cubed tomato and stir well to combine. Cover and refrigerate until ready to serve.

Pan-Seared Oyster Mushrooms with Smoked Tomato Vinaigrette

Extremely versatile, these mushrooms may be served hot, cold or at room temperature and as a salad, vegetable or appetizer. In the summer, grill the mushrooms on the barbecue instead of pan-searing them.

Serves 4-6

4 Tbsp.	olive oil	60 ml
1/2 tsp.	salt	2.5 ml
1/4 tsp.	pepper	1.2 ml
1 Tbsp.	fresh thyme leaves, or 1 tsp. (5 ml) dried	15 ml
2	cloves garlic, minced	2
2 lbs.	large oyster mushrooms, stem end trimmed	900 g
1/2 recipe	Smoked Tomato Vinaigrette, page 40	1/2 recipe

Combine the olive oil, salt, pepper, thyme and garlic in a large bowl. Add the oyster mushrooms and toss well.

Heat a heavy nonstick or well-seasoned frying pan over high heat. Fry half of the mushrooms, pressing them down with a spatula until they are lightly browned. Remove from the pan and repeat with the remaining mushrooms. Return the cooked mushrooms to the pan to heat them through. Transfer to a heated serving platter and drizzle with the smoked tomato vinaigrette.

Warm Chanterelle Salad with Thyme and Rosemary Vinaigrette

Fall is chanterelle time in the Pacific Northwest. This is one of fellow chef Andrew's favorite ways to use them.

Serves 4-6

2 Tbsp.	cider vinegar	30 ml
1 Tbsp.	shallots, finely minced	15 ml
1 tsp.	fresh thyme leaves, chopped	5 ml
1 tsp.	fresh rosemary leaves, chopped	5 ml
1 tsp.	salt	5 ml
1/2 tsp.	black pepper	2.5 ml
1/3 cup	extra virgin olive oil	80 ml
1 lb.	fresh chanterelle or oyster mushrooms	450 g
2 Tbsp.	unsalted butter	30 ml
	salt and pepper to taste	
1	large head escarole, washed, dried and torn into bite-sized pieces	1
1	large bunch of spinach, stemmed, washed and dried	1

Combine the vinegar, shallots, herbs and seasonings in a mixing bowl. Whisk for a few moments to dissolve the salt. Slowly beat in the olive oil.

Clean the chanterelles and tear them into two or four pieces (chanterelles are slightly fibrous and are easily torn). Melt the butter in a frying pan over medium heat and add the chanterelles. Cook, stirring frequently, for about 3 minutes until the mushrooms are soft. Season with salt and pepper.

While the mushrooms are cooking, toss the greens with the vinaigrette and arrange on individual plates or a large platter. When the mushrooms are done, spoon them over the salads and serve immediately.

Chicken Salad with Raspberry and Buckwheat Honey Dressing

You can use any cooked or raw vegetables you like for this summery salad.

Serves 4-6

1/4 lb.	snowpeas, trimmed	115 g
1	head romaine lettuce	1
1 recipe	Raspberry and Buckwheat Honey Dressing, page 39	1 recipe
3 cups	cooked chicken or turkey, boned and cut into 1-inch (2.5-cm) cubes	750 ml
1/4	English cucumber, sliced into half moons	1/4
2	medium tomatoes, cut into 8 wedges each	2
1/2 cup	walnut halves	125 ml

Bring a small pot of water to a boil. Add the snowpeas and cook for a minute or so, until they turn bright green. Drain and cool under cold water. Drain and reserve.

Wash, dry and tear the romaine. Toss with half the dressing and place on a large platter. Arrange the chicken or turkey, cucumber, snowpeas, tomatoes and walnuts on top of the lettuce. Drizzle with the remaining dressing and serve.

Grilled Eggplant Salad with Yogurt Dressing

This is a fantastic summer salad and is also great the next day. Serve it with grilled chicken or as part of an antipasto plate.

Serves 6-8

3 cups	plain yogurt	750 ml
4	small eggplants, about 3 lbs. (1.3 kg)	4
	olive oil	
1/4 cup	water	60 ml
1/2 tsp.	salt	2.5 ml
1/4 tsp.	pepper	1.2 ml
1/4 cup	fresh basil leaves, chopped	60 ml
1/4 cup	fresh mint leaves, chopped	60 ml
2	cloves garlic, minced	2
1	large tomato, finely diced	1

Place the yogurt in a sieve lined with a coffee filter or a double layer of cheesecloth and let it drain over a bowl for 2 hours. Top and tail the eggplants and cut into 3/4-inch (2-cm) slices.

Preheat the barbecue or broiler to medium. Lightly brush both sides of the eggplant slices with olive oil and grill or broil until golden brown on both sides and completely tender, about 4-5 minutes per side. Remove from the heat and arrange attractively on a platter to cool.

When the yogurt has finished draining, place in a bowl and stir in the water, then add the salt, pepper, basil, mint and garlic. Drizzle the dressing over the eggplant and scatter the chopped tomatoes over the top.

Arugula Salad with Warm Bacon and Apple Vinaigrette

If arugula is unavailable, you can substitute watercress or escarole in this recipe.

Serves 4

2	large bunches arugula, trimmed, washed and dried	2
2 Tbsp.	apple cider vinegar	30 ml
1/4 tsp.	salt	1.2 ml
1/4 tsp.	black pepper	1.2 ml
3 Tbsp.	vegetable oil	60 ml
8	slices bacon	8
1	small apple, peeled, cored and thinly sliced	1

Place the arugula in a large bowl. Add the apple cider vinegar, salt and pepper and toss well. Set aside.

Heat the vegetable oil in a frying pan on medium heat. Add the bacon and cook until just crisp. Add the apple slices and heat through.

Pour immediately over the arugula and toss well. Divide among 4 heated plates and serve immediately.

Grilled Summer Vegetables with Sun-Dried Tomato Pesto

These vegetables are an excellent accompaniment to grilled lamb. They can also be the focal point of a meal, served with an assortment of cheeses and a good bread. Leftovers are good cold the next day.

Serves 4-6

1	medium zucchini, trimmed and sliced into 1/4-inch (.5-cm) slices lengthwise	1
1	small eggplant, trimmed and sliced into 1/2-inch (1-cm) slices	1
1/2 lb.	mushrooms	225 g
16	cherry tomatoes	16
1	red onion, peeled and cut into 8 wedges	1
	olive oil	
	salt and pepper to taste	

Preheat the barbecue or broiler on medium heat. Brush all the vegetables lightly with olive oil and season with salt and pepper. Grill or broil the vegetables until tender. Arrange on a large platter and allow to cool.

Before serving, drizzle with the tomato pesto.

Sun-Dried Tomato Pesto

1/2 cup	sun-dried tomatoes (not oil-packed)	125 ml
1 cup	boiling water	250 ml
3	cloves garlic, minced	3
1/2 cup	olive oil	125 ml
1/2 cup	fresh basil leaves, loosely packed	125 ml
	salt and pepper to taste	

Place the sun-dried tomatoes in a bowl and pour the boiling water over them. Let sit for 1 hour. Drain the tomatoes, reserving 1/2 cup (125 ml) of the soaking water.

Place the tomatoes, garlic, oil, basil and the reserved soaking water in a food processor or blender and purée until smooth. Season with salt and pepper.

Beet Salad with Mint and Feta Cheese

If you have access to a farmers' or specialty market you may find that they carry many different varieties of beets. Yellow, white, Chioggia and Easter egg beets are more commonly available now and make a nice change from the purple variety.

Serves 6

1 lb.	small beets	450 g
6 Tbsp.	blackberry or apple cider vinegar	90 ml
2 Tbsp.	honey	30 ml
1/2 tsp.	salt	2.5 ml
1	small onion, thinly sliced	1
3 Tbsp.	coarsely chopped mint	45 ml
1/4 lb.	feta cheese, crumbled	115 g

Place the beets in a pot and cover with water. Bring to a boil, then turn down to a simmer. Cook the beets until they can be pierced easily with the tip of a sharp knife, about 30-40 minutes. Drain.

Combine the vinegar, honey, salt and onion in a wide, shallow bowl. When the beets are cool enough to handle, slip off the skins and cut into 3/8-inch (1-cm) slices. Add to the vinegar mixture and stir well. (The beets may be covered and refrigerated overnight at this point.) Marinate until just before serving. Drain half the dressing from the beets and onions and place them on a plate. Sprinkle with half the mint. Scatter the feta over the beets and sprinkle with the remaining mint.

Spicy Bean and Corn Salad

A great summer salad. Serve it with the Grilled Turkey Breast with Tomato Cumin Vinaigrette, on page 96.

Serves 6-8

1/2 cup	dried black beans	125 ml
1/2 cup	dried kidney beans	125 ml
1/2 cup	dried navy beans	125 ml
1/2 cup	dried chick peas	125 ml
1 recipe	Smoked Tomato Vinaigrette, page 40	1 recipe
1 1/2 cups	corn kernels, fresh or thawed if frozen	375 ml
1	jalepeño pepper, finely diced	1
1/2 cup	thinly sliced green onion	125 ml
1/2 cup	diced celery	125 ml
1/2 cup	coarsely chopped cilantro	125 ml
	salt and pepper to taste	
2	medium, ripe tomatoes, cut into 1/2-inch (1-cm) cubes	2

Cook the dried beans in separate pots until tender but not mushy, 1 1/2-2 hours. Drain each type of bean as it is cooked and place in a large bowl. Toss with the vinaigrette and set aside to cool while you are preparing the other ingredients.

Bring a pot of water to a boil, add the corn and cook until tender, 3-5 minutes. Drain and add to the beans. When the beans and corn have completely cooled, add the jalepeño pepper, green onion, celery and cilantro. Season with salt and pepper. (The salad will taste better if you cover and refrigerate it overnight.) Add the tomatoes just before serving.

New Potato Salad with Yogurt Dressing

Lighter and more refreshing than a traditional mayonnaise-based potato salad.

Serves 4-6

1 1/2 lbs.	new red or white potatoes, skin on, cut into 1-inch (2.5-cm) cubes	675 g
1/4 tsp.	turmeric	1.2 ml
	salt	
1 1/2 cups	plain yogurt	375 ml
4 Tbsp.	Dijon mustard	60 ml
1 1/2 tsp.	whole cumin seeds	7.5 ml
1 Tbsp.	ground coriander seeds	15 ml
	pinch of cayenne pepper	
4	green onions, thinly sliced	4
2 Tbsp.	chopped cilantro	30 ml
	salt and pepper to taste	

Combine the potatoes and turmeric in a large pot and cover with water. Salt well and bring to a boil. Cook until the potatoes are tender but not mushy, about 15 minutes. Drain the potatoes and place in a bowl to cool.

Combine the remaining ingredients and season with salt and pepper. Pour over the cooled potatoes and mix well. Allow 1 hour before serving for the flavors to blend.

Inspired by My Mother's Potato Salad

In the sixties, Dijon mustard was an exotic ingredient, onion flakes were commonplace (still are) and Miracle Whip ruled (still does!). So, while this is not exactly my mother's original potato salad, it has the same sentimental value—and it has my mother's approval.

Serves 4-6

1 1/2 lbs.	medium russet potatoes, skin on	675 g
4	large eggs, hardcooked	4
1 cup	prepared mayonnaise	250 ml
1/2 cup	sour cream	125 ml
2 Tbsp.	Dijon mustard	30 ml
1/2 cup	finely chopped celery	125 ml
1/2 cup	finely sliced green onion	125 ml
	salt and pepper to taste	

Cook the potatoes in boiling water until tender, 30-40 minutes. Drain and let cool completely.

Remove and discard the skin from the potatoes and grate coarsely into a bowl. Peel the eggs and grate over the potatoes. Combine the remaining ingredients and season with salt and pepper. Pour over the potatoes and eggs and mix well. Cover and refrigerate for 1 hour before serving.

Beet Vinaigrette

I love this vinaigrette. Aside from its gorgeous color, it has a subtle sweet and sour flavor and a multitude of uses.

Makes 3/4 cup (185 ml)

2 Tbsp.	cider or white wine vinegar	30 ml
1/2 cup	vegetable oil	125 ml
1/2 tsp.	salt	2.5 ml
1 Tbsp.	honey	15 ml
4 Tbsp.	cooked beet, finely diced	60 ml

Combine the ingredients in a blender or food processor. Process until the beet is puréed. Refrigerate until needed. The vinaigrette keeps for 1 week, refrigerated.

Try this vinaigrette

- on Belgian endive, watercress and smoked salmon salad
- with poached or grilled salmon
- on thinly sliced fennel and shaved asiago
- tossed with cooked and cooled green beans, toasted chopped hazelnuts and crumbled blue cheese
- drizzled on sliced cucumbers, cubed feta, fresh mint and walnuts
- with cooked or grilled asparagus
- tossed with julienned cold roast pork, spinach and toasted sesame seeds

Raspberry and Buckwheat Honey Dressing

This dressing is excellent with chicken, salads or drizzled lightly over fruit salads.

Makes 1 1/4 cups (310 ml)

1 cup	raspberries	250 ml
2 tsp.	buckwheat honey	10 ml
1/2 tsp.	salt	2.5 ml
1 Tbsp.	cider vinegar	15 ml
1 Tbsp.	shallots, finely diced	15 ml
1/2 cup	vegetable oil	125 ml

Place the raspberries in a food processor or blender and purée. Press the purée through a sieve and discard the seeds.

Return the purée to the food processor or blender. Add the honey, salt, vinegar and shallots. With the motor running, add the oil in a slow steady stream. This dressing keeps for 1 month, covered and refrigerated.

Gazpacho Vinaigrette

I use this summery and elegant vinaigrette with steamed clams, or surrounding salmon or halibut, or with a chicken and avocado salad.

Makes 2 1/2 cups (625 ml)

1 lb.	ripe tomatoes, cored and chopped	450 g
1/2	red pepper, seeded and cut into pieces	1/2
1/2	cucumber, peeled, seeded and chopped	1/2
1	clove garlic, minced	1
3 Tbsp.	red wine vinegar	45 ml
3 Tbsp.	olive oil	45 ml
1/2 cup	cold water	125 ml
1/2-1 tsp.	salt	2.5-5 ml
	cayenne pepper to taste	
1 tsp.	sugar	5 ml
2 Tbsp.	finely diced onion	30 ml
1 Tbsp.	finely chopped cilantro	15 ml

Place all the ingredients except the onion and cilantro in a food processor or blender and pulse until the vegetables are almost puréed. Check the seasoning as it will depend on the sweetness of the tomatoes, and adjust it with more salt, sugar and red wine vinegar. (The vinaigrette may be made to this point up to 2 days in advance. Cover and refrigerate.) Stir in the onion and cilantro just before serving.

Smoked Tomato Vinaigrette

An absolutely great vinaigrette. In a restaurant situation it is easy to smoke the tomatoes over alder chips, but it is a somewhat messy and smoky process to go through at home. I have cheated here and used canned tomatoes and liquid smoke with no apologies. The results are superb.

Makes 1 1/4 cups (310 ml)

6	canned plum tomatoes, well drained	6
2 tsp.	cider vinegar	10 ml
1/8 tsp.	pepper	.5 ml
1/4 tsp.	liquid smoke	1.2 ml
1	medium clove garlic, minced	1
1/2 tsp.	salt	2.5 ml
1/2 cup	olive oil	125 ml

Combine the tomatoes, vinegar, pepper and liquid smoke in a food processor or blender. Mash the garlic to a paste with some of the salt. Add the garlic along with the remaining salt to the ingredients and blend until puréed. With the motor on, add the olive oil in a slow steady stream. Store covered and refrigerated for up to 3 weeks.

Use this vinaigrette as a salad dressing or

- with grilled oyster mushrooms
- as a marinade for chicken
- on a pasta salad made with orzo, prawns and roasted red peppers
- with salmon, snapper or halibut
- with grilled calamari
- tossed with warm, cooked black beans
- with freshly cooked green beans or corn

PACIFIC PASSIONS
Pasta
and
Pizza

Spaghettini with Calamari, Chilies and Aioli

The aioli combines beautifully with the spicy tomato sauce.

Be careful not to overcook the calamari.

Serves 4 as a main course, 6 as an appetizer

1	28-oz. (796-ml) can plum tomatoes	1
4 Tbsp.	olive oil	60 ml
1/2 cup	finely diced onion	125 ml
1/8 tsp.	chili flakes, or to taste	.5 ml
	salt and pepper to taste	
1 lb.	small calamari, cleaned	450 g
1 lb.	dried spaghettini	450 g

To make the sauce, purée the tomatoes in a food processor or blender and strain through a sieve to remove the seeds. Heat the olive oil in a saucepan over medium heat and sauté the onion until translucent. Add the strained tomatoes and chili flakes. Simmer the sauce until it is reduced by one-third, about 20-30 minutes. Season with salt and pepper and remove from the heat. Slice the calamari tubes into 1/4-inch (.5-cm) rings and the tentacles in half. Refrigerate until ready to use.

Bring a large pot of water to a boil and salt liberally. Add the pasta and cook until tender but still firm to the bite. While the pasta is cooking, slowly reheat the sauce. When the pasta is cooked, quickly drain it and return to the pot. Add the tomato sauce and calamari. Toss over medium heat until the calamari becomes opaque. Serve immediately in heated bowls with aioli on the side.

Aioli

1	medium clove garlic, minced	1
1/4 tsp.	salt	1.2 ml
1/3 cup	olive oil	80 ml
1/3 cup	vegetable oil	80 ml
1	large egg yolk	1
2-3 tsp.	lemon juice	10-15 ml

Crush the garlic to a paste with the salt. Blend the oils together. Using a whisk or a hand mixer, beat the egg yolk and garlic paste together. Slowly dribble in the oil, beating constantly to form an emulsion. When all of the oil has been incorporated, add the lemon juice. (The aioli may be made up to 3 days in advance. Cover and refrigerate.)

Linguine with Manila Clams and Corn

The sweetness of the corn and the saltiness of the clams sing out in harmony. This is another of my favorite pastas.

Much to his disappointment, the only thing my husband, Steven, can't eat is clams. On nights when he was working and I wasn't, I would buy clams and make a great clam linguine for myself. It always makes me feel naughty, relishing this dish that I cannot share with him—and especially naughty if I eat it with someone else.

Serves 2 as a main course, 4 as an appetizer

1 1/2 lbs.	Manila clams, scrubbed	675 g
2 Tbsp.	water	30 ml
1/3 cup	olive oil	80 ml
2	medium cloves garlic, peeled and thinly sliced	2
1/2 cup	white wine	125 ml
1 Tbsp.	finely chopped parsley	15 ml
1/8 tsp.	chili flakes, or to taste (see Chili Flakes, page 45)	.5 ml
1/2 lb.	dried linguine	225 g
1	ear of corn, kernels cut off, about 1/2 cup (125 ml)	1
4 Tbsp.	freshly grated Parmesan cheese	60 ml

Place the clams and water in a pot with a tight-fitting lid. Cook over high heat until the clams open. Remove from the heat. When the clams are cool enough to handle, remove them from their shells and swish them around in the clam liquor to remove any sand. Chop the clams coarsely. Strain the liquor through a coffee filter or paper towels to remove any sand, reserving the liquor.

Heat the olive oil over medium heat and sauté the sliced garlic until golden. Add the white wine and cook until reduced by half. Add the clam liquor and reduce by half again. Remove from the heat and stir in the clams, parsley and chili flakes.

Bring a large pot of water to a boil. Salt liberally and add the linguine. When the water returns to a boil add the corn cob and corn kernels. Cook until the pasta is tender but firm to the bite. Drain and return the pasta to the pot, discarding the corn cob. Quickly reheat the sauce and toss with the pasta over low heat until evenly coated. Add the Parmesan cheese and toss a few more times. Serve immediately in heated bowls.

Seashell Pasta with Tomatoes, Bocconcini, Prawns and Basil

This pasta captures the essence of late summer. Tomatoes, prawns and basil are at their best and the bocconcini is ripe on the vine. Ha!

Serves 4 as a main course, 6 as an appetizer

1 1/2 lbs.	ripe plum tomatoes	675 g
2	cloves garlic, cut in half and lightly crushed	2
1/3 cup	extra virgin olive oil	80 ml
3/4 tsp.	salt	4 ml
1/2 tsp.	coarsely ground black pepper	2.5 ml
2	good-quality bocconcini	2
1/2 cup	fresh basil leaves, loosely packed	125 ml
1 lb.	large prawns or shrimp, peeled and deveined	450 g
1 lb.	medium-sized seashell pasta	450 g

Peel and seed the tomatoes (see Two Ways to Peel a Tomato, page 128). Dice them and place in a bowl.

Skewer the garlic on a toothpick (this will make it easier to retrieve later) and add to the tomatoes. Mix in the olive oil, salt and pepper. Dice the bocconcini. Tear the basil into small pieces. Add these to the tomatoes and stir well. Let the whole mixture marinate for at least an hour, or up to 4 hours.

Cut the prawns or shrimp into 3 pieces crosswise and refrigerate until ready to serve.

Bring a large pot of water to a boil. Salt liberally and add the pasta. Cook until tender but firm to the bite. Drain and return to the pot over medium heat. Remove the garlic from the tomatoes. Add the prawns and the tomato sauce to the pasta. Stir gently until the prawn pieces are cooked through and the bocconcini starts to melt. Serve immediately in warm bowls.

Spaghetti with Prawns and Chorizo Sausage

This is one of my favorite pastas. Pork and shellfish may seem like a novel combination, but it has ancient roots in Portugal and Spain. History aside, it is utterly delicious.

Serves 4-6

20	large prawns	20
12 oz.	raw, unsmoked, chorizo sausage	350 g
3 Tbsp.	extra virgin olive oil	45 ml
1/4 cup	finely diced onion	60 ml
3	medium cloves garlic, minced	3
1/2 cup	white wine	125 ml
2	28-oz. (796-ml) cans plum tomatoes, drained, puréed and sieved to remove the seeds	2
	dried chili flakes to taste	
	salt and pepper to taste	
1 lb.	dried spaghetti	450 g

Peel the prawns and reserve the shells. You may leave the prawns whole (nice to look at) or cut them in half crosswise (easier to eat). Refrigerate the prawns. Place the shells in a small pot. Cover with 2 cups (500 ml) of water and bring to a boil. Reduce the heat and simmer 20 minutes. Remove from the heat and strain, reserving the stock.

While the prawn stock is simmering, remove the sausages from their casings and crumble. Heat the oil in a pot over medium heat and sauté the onion and garlic until the garlic starts to turn golden. Add the crumbled sausage and cook until the sausage loses its raw appearance. Add the white wine and prawn stock. Cook at a rapid boil, watching the sauce carefully. As soon as you see the oil starting to float on top of the sauce, remove from the heat. Add the tomatoes and turn the heat down to medium low. Simmer the sauce until it heavily coats the back of a spoon, 15-20 minutes. Season to taste with the chili flakes, salt and pepper. Remove from the heat.

Bring a large pot of water to a boil, salt well and add the spaghetti. Cook until tender but firm to the bite. A few minutes before the pasta is done, reheat the sauce. Drain the pasta and return it to the pot it was cooked in, add the sauce and the prawns, and stir for a few minutes on low heat until the prawns are cooked through. Serve immediately in heated bowls.

Chili Flakes

I like to make chili flakes by dry-roasting and grinding whole dried chilies. To do this, take a handful of dried chilies and remove any stems. Heat a heavy frying pan over medium heat and dry-roast the chilies along with a teaspoonful (5 ml) of salt, stirring constantly until the peppers turn dark brown. Keep your hood fan on to remove the nose- and eye-tingling perfume of roasting chilies! Cool the chilies on a plate. When cool, grind to a coarse powder in a coffee grinder or spice mill.

These nutty-flavored and aromatic chili flakes are a far cry from the commonly available, caustic chili flakes sold in stores. They can be used in any recipe that calls for chili flakes.

Linguine for Sharon with Prawns, Tomatoes, Black Beans and Chilies

The beautiful and gracious Sharon works with my husband. She is an enthusiastic supporter of good food, good wine and great service. This is one of her favorite pasta dishes.

The fermented black beans give this sauce an intriguing earthy flavor that is complemented by the sweetness of the prawns and the bite of the chilies.

Serves 4 as a main course, 6 as an appetizer

6 Tbsp.	olive oil	90 ml
1/2 cup	finely diced onion	125 ml
2	medium cloves garlic, minced	2
1 1/2	28-oz. (796-ml) cans tomatoes, well drained of juice	1 1/2
1/8 tsp.	chili flakes, or to taste (see Chili Flakes, page 45)	.5 ml
2 Tbsp.	fermented black beans*	30 ml
1 lb.	dried linguine	450 g
	salt to taste	
1/2 lb.	medium prawns, peeled and cut into 3 pieces each	225 g

*Available at Oriental markets and well-stocked supermarkets.

Heat the oil in a saucepan over medium heat and sauté the onions and garlic until the onions are translucent. Finely chop the tomatoes and add to the onions along with the chili flakes. Simmer until the sauce thickens, about 20-30 minutes. Add the black beans and remove from the heat.

Bring a large pot of water to a boil. Salt liberally and add the pasta. Cook until tender but still firm to the bite. Slowly reheat the sauce while the pasta is cooking. Check for seasoning and add salt and more chili flakes if you like. Drain the pasta and place back into the pot. Add the sauce and the prawns. Toss over medium heat until the prawns are cooked through, 3-4 minutes. Serve immediately in heated bowls.

Penne with Butternut Squash, Capers and Raisins

This has a subtle sweet and sour flavor that is utterly delicious. You can use cauliflower, broken into small florets, in place of the squash.

Try serving this pasta with grated Pecorino Romano instead of Parmesan. It is a robustly flavored grating cheese found in large supermarkets and Italian delicatessens.

Serves 4-6

1 1/2 cups	butternut squash, peeled and diced into 3/8-inch (1-cm) cubes	375 ml
6 Tbsp.	olive oil	90 ml
2	medium cloves garlic, minced	2
1/4 cup	finely diced onion	60 ml
1	dried red chili pepper, crumbled	1
1	28-oz. (796-ml) can plum tomatoes, coarsely chopped, with their juice	1
2 Tbsp.	golden raisins	30 ml
1 Tbsp.	capers	15 ml
	salt and pepper to taste	
1 lb.	dried penne	450 g
1/2 cup	grated Parmesan cheese	125 ml

Bring a small pot of water to a boil. Add a pinch of salt and the butternut squash. Cook until tender but not mushy, about 10-15 minutes. Drain.

Heat the olive oil in a saucepan over medium heat. Sauté the garlic, onion and chili pepper until the garlic turns a pale golden color. Add the tomatoes, raisins and capers. Bring to a boil, then reduce the heat to a simmer. Cook until the sauce reduces by half and is thick, about 20-30 minutes. Season with salt and pepper. Add the squash and remove from the heat.

Bring a large pot of water to a boil. Add the penne and salt liberally. Cook until tender but firm. Quickly reheat the sauce. Drain the penne and return to the pot. Add the sauce and stir over high heat to coat the pasta with the sauce. Serve immediately in heated bowls with Parmesan cheese.

Baked Orzo and Eggplant with Zucchini and Ricotta Crust

A great make-ahead dish, suitable for buffets or potluck parties.

Serves 8

2 lbs.	eggplant, peeled and sliced into 1-inch-thick (2.5-cm) slices	900 g
	olive oil	
2 Tbsp.	olive oil	30 ml
2/3 cup	finely diced onion	160 ml
2	cloves garlic, minced	2
1	28-oz. (796-ml) can plum tomatoes, coarsely chopped, with their juice	1
2	large pinches cinnamon	2
	salt and pepper to taste	
2 cups	orzo	500 ml
3/4 cup	freshly grated Parmesan cheese	185 ml

Zucchini and Ricotta Crust

1 1/2 lbs.	zucchini, grated	675 g
1 Tbsp.	unsalted butter	15 ml
2 cups	ricotta cheese	500 ml
2	large eggs	2
1/4 tsp.	salt	1.2 ml
	a few gratings of nutmeg	
1/4 cup	freshly grated Parmesan cheese	60 ml
	paprika	

Preheat the broiler. Lightly brush both sides of the eggplant with olive oil. Place on a baking sheet and broil until soft and browned. Cool and cut into quarters.

To make the sauce, heat the 2 Tbsp. (30 ml) olive oil in a medium-sized saucepan over medium heat. Add the onion and garlic and sauté until the onions are golden around the edges. Add the tomatoes and turn the heat down to simmer. Cook for about 20 minutes, until the sauce is thickened. Add the cinnamon and season with salt and pepper. Remove from the heat.

Bring a large pot of water to a boil and salt liberally. Cook the orzo until tender. Drain and stir into the tomato sauce along with the Parmesan cheese. Fold the eggplant into the orzo mixture. Spread into an oiled 9- by 13-inch (22- by 33-cm) baking dish.

To make the topping, squeeze the water out of the zucchini with your hands. Melt the butter in a large frying pan over medium heat. Sauté the zucchini until translucent. Transfer to a sieve and press out more liquid with the back of a spoon.

Place the ricotta in a bowl and beat it briefly with a whisk to loosen it. Beat in the eggs, salt, nutmeg, Parmesan and zucchini. Spread over the orzo mixture. Trace lines of paprika in a diamond pattern over the topping.

Bake for 40 minutes in a preheated 350°F (180°C) oven. Let stand for 10 minutes before cutting.

Fettucine with Asparagus and Lemon

I love this combination. It is a perfect way to show off the first asparagus of spring.

Serves 4 as an appetizer, 2 as a main course

4 Tbsp.	unsalted butter	60 ml
1 1/2 cups	whipping cream	375 ml
2 Tbsp.	lemon juice	60 ml
	finely grated zest of 4 lemons	
	salt and pepper to taste	
1 lb.	fresh fettucine or 1/2 lb. (225 g) dried	450 g
1/2 lb.	fresh asparagus, trimmed and cut into 1-inch (2.5-cm) pieces on the diagonal	225 g
1/2 cup	freshly grated Parmesan cheese	125 ml

Combine the butter and whipping cream in a heavy saucepan. Bring to a boil and add the lemon juice and zest. Continue boiling until the cream is reduced by one-third. Season with salt and pepper and remove from the heat.

Bring a large pot of water to a boil. Salt liberally. If you are using fresh pasta, add the asparagus to the water with the pasta. If using dried pasta, add the asparagus 2 minutes before the pasta is done. Drain the pasta and asparagus.

Reheat the sauce and add the pasta and asparagus, turning it to coat it well with the sauce. Add the Parmesan cheese and stir until the cheese is incorporated. Serve immediately in heated bowls.

Macaroni and Cheese

For some, macaroni and cheese is the ultimate in comfort food. One of my dear friend Bob's favorite comfort dinners is this macaroni and cheese with baked potatoes and sour cream on the side. Not your everyday kind of dinner, mind you, but fitting when extra special cheering up is required!

Serves 6

3 cups	elbow macaroni	750 ml
4 cups	homogenized milk	1 L
4 Tbsp.	butter	60 ml
4 Tbsp.	flour	60 ml
1 tsp.	salt	5 ml
4 cups	grated aged cheddar, loosely packed	1 L
1 1/2 cups	grated aged gouda, loosely packed	375 ml
2 cups	grated medium gouda, loosely packed	500 ml
4 Tbsp.	unsalted butter	60 ml
2 cups	soft white bread crumbs	500 ml

Bring a large pot of water to a boil and salt liberally. Cook the elbow macaroni until tender and drain. Cool under cold running water. Drain and set aside.

Scald the milk. Melt the butter over medium heat. Add the flour and stir for a few minutes. Slowly whisk in the milk and bring to a boil. Reduce the heat to a simmer and cook for 10 minutes, stirring occasionally. Remove from the heat and whisk in the salt, cheddar and aged gouda. Fold in the cooked macaroni.

Butter a 2-quart (2-L) casserole dish. Add half the macaroni and cheese mixture. Cover with the grated medium gouda. Add the rest of the macaroni and cheese. (The casserole can be made up to this point a day in advance. Cover and refrigerate overnight. Increase the baking time to 1 hour and 15 minutes.)

Melt the butter for the crumb topping. Toss with the bread crumbs. Sprinkle on top of the macaroni and cheese. Bake in a preheated 350°F (180°C) oven for 40 minutes until browned and bubbly.

Soft Bread Crumbs

Use a loaf of bread that still has a bit of verve to it, remove the crusts and cut into 1-inch (2.5-cm) cubes. Pulse in small batches in a food processor into coarse crumbs.

Baked Ziti and Cauliflower with Smoked Mozzarella

This is what happens to macaroni and cheese when it goes to heaven. I don't recommend that this dish be made in advance. The beauty of its creamy, cheesy texture is lost if refrigerated and then heated.

There are two types of ziti. One is cut into 2-inch (5-cm) lengths like a jumbo macaroni and the other is the same length as spaghetti. I like to use the long version. It's more fun to cook with and eat.

Serves 6-8

1	large cauliflower, trimmed and cut into 1-inch (2.5-cm) florets	1
1 lb.	ziti	450 g
1	28-oz. (796-ml) can plum tomatoes, well drained and coarsely chopped	1
2 cups	whipping cream	500 ml
	salt and pepper to taste	
3/4 lb.	fontina cheese, grated	350 g
6 oz.	smoked mozzarella, grated	180 g

Bring a large pot of generously salted water (one that will be large enough to cook the ziti in) to a boil. Add the cauliflower and cook until tender-crisp. Remove with a skimmer or slotted spoon and drain. Add the ziti to the pot and cook until tender. Drain and place in a large bowl with the cauliflower.

While the ziti is cooking, combine the tomatoes and cream in a saucepan. Bring to a boil and remove from the heat. Season with salt and pepper and toss with the ziti and cauliflower. Add the grated cheeses and toss again.

Preheat the oven to 350°F (180°C). Place the ziti mixture in a shallow, 6-quart (6-L) casserole dish. Cover with tin foil or a lid and bake for 30 minutes. Remove the cover and bake for 15 minutes longer. Remove from the oven and let rest for 10 minutes before serving.

Basic Pizza Dough

This dough can be jazzed up by the addition of fresh herbs, such as rosemary or thyme. For the sake of convenience, the dough can be left in the fridge to rise for up to 8 hours. I like to put it in a large, oiled, plastic bag and tie the top securely. This will prevent it from escaping and taking over the fridge.

Makes 1 16-inch (40-cm) pizza

1 1/2 cups	lukewarm water	375 ml
1 tsp.	granulated sugar	5 ml
1 Tbsp.	yeast	15 ml
1/4 cup	olive oil	60 ml
1/2 tsp.	salt	2.5 ml
2 1/2-3 cups	unbleached white flour, plus more for kneading	625-750 ml

Combine the water and sugar in a large bowl. Sprinkle the yeast over the surface and let work for 10 minutes.

Stir in the olive oil and salt. Beat in the flour 1 cup (250 ml) at a time until the dough is too hard to beat. Sprinkle about 1 cup (250 ml) of flour onto a flat surface. Scrape the dough out of the bowl and knead it, adding flour as necessary until the dough is smooth and resilient to the touch, about 10 minutes.

Place the dough in a large bowl and pour a bit of olive oil over it. Roll the dough around the bowl to coat it thoroughly with the oil. Cover loosely with plastic wrap or a clean cloth and let rise in a warm place until doubled in bulk, about 2 hours.

Punch down the dough. Lightly oil a 16-inch (40-cm) pizza pan. Roll out and press the dough onto the pan. Proceed with your favorite topping and bake.

Sweet Onion Pizza

Serve this pizza at room temperature as part of an antipasto or with a hearty soup.

Makes 1 16-inch (40-cm) pizza

1 recipe	Basic Pizza Dough, opposite	1 recipe
3 Tbsp.	olive oil	45 ml
4	medium cloves garlic, minced	4
8 cups	very thinly sliced onions	2 L
2	sprigs fresh thyme	2
	salt and pepper to taste	
12	thin slices onion	12

While the pizza dough is rising, prepare the topping. Heat the olive oil in a large frying pan over medium heat and sauté the garlic until golden. Add the 8 cups (2 L) of onions and sauté until translucent. Add the thyme. Cook over low heat, stirring frequently, until the onions have reduced to a soft, light brown mass, about 45 minutes to 1 hour. Remove the thyme sprigs and season with salt and pepper. Remove from the heat.

Preheat the oven to 400°F (200°C). Press the pizza dough into a pizza pan, making a 1/2-inch (1-cm) rim of dough at the edge of the pan.

Spread the cooked onions evenly over the pizza dough. Decorate the top with the thin slices of raw onion. Place in the oven and bake until the dough can be easily removed from the pan, about 10-15 minutes. Slide the pizza off the pan and directly onto the oven rack. Bake until golden brown on the bottom, about 15-20 minutes. Remove from the oven and let rest for 10 minutes before cutting.

Fresh Manila Clam Pizza

This pizza illustrates that the simplest ingredients, thoughtfully combined, can create the best possible things to eat. For the best impression, eat it by itself, while watching the sunset.

Makes 1 16-inch (40-cm) pizza

1 recipe	Basic Pizza Dough, page 52	1 recipe
2 lbs.	Manila clams, scrubbed	900 g
1/4 cup	water	60 ml
1/4 cup.	olive oil	60 ml
2	medium cloves garlic, minced	2
1/4 cup	white wine	60 ml
2 Tbsp.	parsley, finely chopped	30 ml
1/8 tsp.	chili flakes	.5 ml
4 Tbsp.	freshly grated Parmesan cheese	60 ml

While the pizza dough is rising, prepare the topping. Place the clams and water in a pot with a tight-fitting lid. Cook over high heat until the clams open. Remove from the heat. When the clams are cool enough to handle, remove them from their shells and swish them around in the clam liquor to remove any sand. Chop the clams coarsely. Strain the liquor through a coffee filter or paper towels to remove any sand. Reserve the clams and liquor.

Heat the olive oil over medium heat and sauté the garlic until golden. Add the white wine and cook until it is reduced by half. Add the clam liquor and cook until reduced by half. Remove from the heat and add the parsley and chili flakes.

Preheat the oven to 400°F (200°C). Press the pizza dough into an oiled pizza pan, making deep indentations with your fingers. Place in the oven and bake for 10 minutes, until the dough will slide easily off the pan. Spread the clam liquor mixture evenly over the dough. Slide directly onto the oven rack and bake for about 15 minutes, until the bottom of the pizza is lightly browned.

Spread the clams and Parmesan cheese over the crust and bake for 5 minutes more. Remove from the oven and let rest for 5 minutes before cutting.

Spicy Corn and Hand-Peeled Shrimp Pizza

Tiny, sweet, hand-peeled shrimp are another local delicacy. They are a perfect match for sweet summer corn and tomatoes. If they are not available in your area you can use small cooked shrimp.

Makes 1 16-inch (40-cm) pizza

1 recipe	Basic Pizza Dough, page 52	1 recipe
2	large ripe tomatoes, thinly sliced	2
1/2 tsp.	salt	2.5 ml
2	ears of fresh corn	2
2	cloves garlic, thinly sliced	2
1/2 lb.	hand-peeled shrimp, well drained	225 g
1/2	jalapeño pepper, finely chopped	1/2
12 oz.	mozzarella cheese, grated	350 g

While the pizza dough is rising, prepare the topping. Thinly slice the tomatoes and place in a single layer on a platter. Sprinkle with the salt and let sit for 1/2 hour.

While the tomatoes are sitting, bring a small pot of water to a boil. Cut the kernels from the ears of corn and add to the water. Cook until tender, 3-5 minutes. Drain and reserve.

Preheat the oven to 400°F (200°C). Press the pizza dough into a lightly oiled pizza pan. Drain the juice from the tomatoes and place the tomatoes on the dough. Sprinkle with the sliced garlic. Place in the oven and bake for about 10 minutes, until the pizza can be easily slipped off the pan.

Combine the hand-peeled shrimp, corn, jalapeño and mozzarella. Transfer the pizza directly onto the oven rack and sprinkle with the mozzarella cheese mixture. Bake until golden brown on the bottom, about 15-20 minutes. Remove from the oven and let rest 10 minutes before cutting.

Beet Green Pizza with Garlic and Mozzarella

As a lover of beet greens, I am always searching for new ways to use them. This shows them off beautifully. A hearty green, such as Swiss chard or mustard greens, can be substituted if you like.

Makes 1 16-inch (40-cm) pizza

1 recipe	Basic Pizza Dough, page 52	1 recipe
1 lb.	beet greens with stems removed, washed and drained	450 g
4 Tbsp.	olive oil	60 ml
2	medium cloves garlic, minced	2
	salt and pepper to taste	
12 oz.	mozzarella cheese, grated	350 g

While the pizza dough is rising, prepare the topping. Steam the beet greens in a large lidded pot over high heat, stirring occasionally until they are tender, 3-5 minutes. Drain and spread on a tray to cool. When they are cool enough to handle, squeeze the water out with your hands and chop finely.

Heat the olive oil over medium heat and sauté the garlic until light golden. Add the beet greens and toss to coat with the olive oil and garlic. Season with the salt and pepper and remove from the heat.

Preheat the oven to 400°F (200°C). Press the pizza dough into a pizza pan. Spread the beet greens evenly over the dough. Bake for about 10 minutes, until the pizza can be slipped off the pan easily. Sprinkle the pizza with mozzarella cheese and transfer the pizza directly onto the oven rack. Bake until golden brown on the bottom, about 15-20 minutes. Remove from the oven and let rest 10 minutes before cutting.

Fish and Shellfish

Cornmeal Fried Oysters with Red Cabbage, Sausage and Garlic Mayonnaise

A warming late fall or winter dish, when oysters and red cabbage are at their best. Pass the garlic mayonnaise separately.

Serves 4

4 cups	red cabbage, cored and thinly sliced, approximately 1 lb. (450 g)	1 L
3 Tbsp.	apple cider vinegar	45 ml
1/2 tsp	salt	2.5 ml
1 tsp.	sugar	5 ml
2 Tbsp.	vegetable oil	30 ml
2	cloves garlic, minced	2
1	small onion, finely diced	1
2	hot Italian sausages, approximately 1/2 lb. (225 g), skinned	2
1/2	apple, peeled, cored and thinly sliced	1/2
2/3 cup	flour	160 ml
1/3 cup	cornmeal	80 ml
1/2 tsp.	salt	2.5 ml
1/2 tsp.	black pepper	2.5 ml
1/4 tsp.	turmeric	1.2 ml
	large pinch cayenne pepper	
20	medium shucked oysters, well drained, approximately 1 lb. (500 g)	20
	vegetable oil for frying	

Toss the red cabbage, vinegar, salt and sugar. Set aside while you are preparing the other ingredients.

Heat the 2 Tbsp. (30 ml) oil in a large heavy frying pan over medium heat and sauté the garlic until light gold in color. Stir in the onion and sauté until lightly browned. Add the sausages and fry, crumbling with a fork, until cooked through. Add the apple and the red cabbage mixture and turn the heat to high. Sauté, stirring frequently, until the cabbage is glistening and heated through. Remove from the heat.

Mix the flour, cornmeal, salt, pepper, turmeric and cayenne pepper together. Spread out on a large plate.

Coat the oysters with the cornmeal mixture and place on a plate. Sprinkle the leftover cornmeal mixture over the oysters.

Preheat the oven to 250°F (120°C). Heat 1/2 inch (1 cm) vegetable oil in a large, heavy frying pan until a haze forms over the oil (325°F/160°C). Fry the oysters, without overcrowding the pan, until golden brown on both sides. Drain each batch on absorbent paper, then transfer to a baking sheet and place in the oven.

When the oysters are all cooked, reheat the cabbage and sausage mixture over high heat, stirring frequently, until hot and tender-crisp. Place on a heated platter and surround with the oysters.

Garlic Mayonnaise

1	egg yolk	1
1 tsp.	Dijon mustard	5 ml
1/2 cup	vegetable oil	125 ml
1/2 cup	olive oil	125 ml
4 tsp.	lemon juice	20 ml
1	large clove garlic, finely chopped then mashed to a paste with 1/2 tsp. (2.5 ml) salt	1

Combine the egg yolk and mustard in the work bowl of a food processor. With the motor running, slowly dribble in the olive and vegetable oils. Add the lemon juice and garlic with salt and pulse a few times to combine. Transfer to a bowl, cover and refrigerate for up to 2 days.

Purist's Oyster Stew

Eat this on a cold rainy day with a still-warm loaf of soda bread and you will feel contentment right down to your toes.

Serves 2 as a main course

1 pt.	shucked oysters with their juice	500 ml
2 cups	homogenized milk	500 ml
1 1/2 cups	half-and-half cream	375 ml
	a few drops Tabasco sauce	
	a few drops Worcestershire sauce	
	salt and pepper to taste	
	unsalted butter	

If the oysters are large, cut them into quarters.

Heat the milk and cream in a saucepan until just steaming. In another pan, heat the oysters with their juice just until their edges curl up. Pour the steaming milk and cream over the oysters and heat until very hot but not boiling.

Season to taste with Tabasco and Worcestershire sauce, salt and pepper. Serve in large heated bowls, with a piece of butter floating on top.

Oyster Stew with Chorizo Sausage and Spinach

While not as pure as the previous oyster stew, it is pretty darned delicious. Serve it with Beer Bread, page 179.

Serves 4

1 Tbsp.	vegetable oil	15 ml
2	chorizo sausages, skinned and crumbled	2
1/2 cup	finely chopped onion	125 ml
2 cups	homogenized milk	500 ml
1 1/2 cups	half-and-half cream	375 ml
1/2 lb.	spinach, stems removed, washed and finely chopped	225 g
1 pt.	shucked oysters with their juice, cut into quarters if large	500 ml
	a few drops Tabasco sauce	
	a few drops Worcestershire sauce	
	salt and pepper to taste	

Heat the vegetable oil in a large pot over medium heat. Add the sausage and onion and cook, crumbling the sausage until it turns brown. Drain to remove the oil and return to the pot.

Add the milk and cream to the pot and heat until just steaming. Add the spinach and simmer for a minute or two. In another pan, heat the oysters with their juice just until their edges curl up. Pour the oysters into the steaming milk and cream, and heat until very hot but not boiling.

Season to taste with Tabasco and Worcestershire sauce, salt and pepper. Serve in large heated bowls.

Stir-Fried Prawns with Asparagus

Fast, easy, and great to cook in spring when local prawns and asparagus are in season.

Serves 3-4

1 lb.	large prawns or shrimp, peeled	450 g
1/2 tsp.	salt	2.5 ml
1/2 lb.	asparagus, woody ends snapped off	225 g
4	green onions	4
2 Tbsp.	vegetable oil	30 ml
10	thin slices peeled ginger	10
1 Tbsp.	Chinese cooking wine or dry sherry	15 ml
1/4 tsp.	salt	1.2 ml
1/2 tsp.	sugar	2.5 ml
1 tsp.	sesame oil	5 ml

Mix the prawns or shrimp with the 1/2 tsp. (2.5 ml) salt. Cover and refrigerate for 1 hour.

Cut the asparagus into 1 1/2-inch (4-cm) diagonal pieces. Cut the green onions into 2-inch (5-cm) lengths.

Heat a wok or large frying pan over high heat. Add the oil, then the ginger. As soon as it sizzles, add the asparagus and stir-fry until it turns bright green. Add the prawns or shrimp and stir-fry until they are almost done, 2-3 minutes. Mix in the green onions, cooking wine or sherry, salt, sugar and sesame oil. Give it a few more stirs and serve immediately.

Shrimp Pad Thai

This is a great way of using our local hand-peeled shrimp and a cooking-class favorite; the spicy sweet-sour flavor has universal appeal. Many people have confessed to making extra so they can eat it cold out of the fridge the next day!

Serves 4

1/2 lb.	medium-width rice noodles* (look for Erewan Brand in the blue package)	250 g
2 Tbsp.	oyster sauce*	30 ml
4 Tbsp.	ketchup	60 ml
2 Tbsp.	molasses	30 ml
2 Tbsp.	sugar	30 ml
2 Tbsp.	fish sauce*	30 ml
4 Tbsp.	water	60 ml
1 tsp.	dried chili flakes	5 ml
1/4 cup	vegetable oil	60 ml
6	cloves garlic, minced	6
2	eggs	2
1 1/2 cups	cooked shrimp	375 ml
2 cups	bean sprouts	500 ml
2 cups	Chinese chives cut into 1-inch (2.5-cm) lengths or green onions	500 ml
2 Tbsp.	chopped roasted peanuts	30 ml
	cilantro sprigs	

*Available at Oriental markets and well-stocked supermarkets.

Place the rice noodles in a bowl and cover with warm water for 30 minutes. Combine the oyster sauce, ketchup, molasses, sugar, fish sauce, water and chili flakes in a small bowl and set aside.

Heat the vegetable oil in a wok or large frying pan over high heat. Stir-fry the garlic until golden. Add the eggs and scramble until dry. Drain the noodles and add them to the pan. Stir-fry until the noodles soften, become shiny and start sticking together in a mass. This is crucial to the texture of the finished dish. Add the shrimp, bean sprouts, chives or green onions and the sauce. Cook until the sauce is absorbed. Turn out onto a platter and garnish with the peanuts and cilantro.

Grilled Prawns with Three Dipping Sauces

Sweet, plump Pacific prawns with black bean mayonnaise, smoked tomato vinaigrette and chive butter: this dish was picked as most memorable meal by an editor of* Gourmet Magazine. *I must confess, its fans are legion.

Serves 4

2 lbs.	large prawns or shrimp, peeled	900 g
	salt and pepper to taste	
1 Tbsp.	vegetable oil	15 ml
1 recipe	Smoked Tomato Vinaigrette, page 40	1 recipe
1 cup	mayonnaise	250 ml
1 Tbsp.	sesame oil	15 ml
2 tsp.	lemon juice	10 ml
2 Tbsp.	Chinese fermented black beans*	30 ml
1/2 cup	unsalted butter	125 ml
1/4 tsp.	salt	1.2 ml
2 tsp.	coarsely ground black pepper	10 ml
3 Tbsp.	chives or green onions, minced	45 ml

*Available at Oriental markets and well-stocked supermarkets.

Liberally salt and pepper the prawns. Toss with the vegetable oil. Thread the prawns on 4 skewers. (Use metal skewers or wooden ones that have been presoaked in water for half an hour.) Refrigerate until ready to cook.

Make the smoked tomato vinaigrette.

To make the black bean mayonnaise, combine the mayonnaise, sesame oil, lemon juice, and black beans in the work bowl of a food processor or blender. Pulse until the beans are finely chopped. (To make it by hand, finely chop the beans on a cutting board, then mash them to a paste with the flat of a knife. Place in a bowl with the sesame oil and lemon juice and whisk until smooth. Whisk in the mayonnaise.) Refrigerate until ready to serve.

To make chive butter, melt the butter over low heat. Add the salt and pepper, remove from the heat and add chives or green onions.

Preheat the barbecue or broiler. Grill or broil the prawns for 2-3 minutes on each side until just cooked through. Transfer to a heated platter and serve immediately with the sauces.

Dungeness Crab Cakes

This is my husband's recipe. These are creamy cakes with sweet russets of crab. Serve with cocktail sauce, tartar sauce, or the Sweet and Sour Cucumber-Beer Relish for red snapper, page 75.

Makes 12 crab cakes

5 Tbsp.	unsalted butter	75 ml
1/4 cup	finely chopped onion	60 ml
1/4 cup	finely chopped celery	60 ml
3/4 cup	milk	185 ml
6 Tbsp.	flour	90 ml
2	large egg yolks	2
1/2 tsp.	salt	2.5 ml
	pepper to taste	
8 drops	Tabasco sauce	8 drops
2 tsp.	finely chopped parsley	10 ml
12 oz.	Dungeness crab meat, picked over and squeezed dry	350 g
1 1/2 cups	bread crumbs	375 ml
1	large egg	1
2 Tbsp.	water	30 ml
1 cup	flour	250 ml
	vegetable oil for frying	

Melt the butter in a saucepan over low heat. Sauté the onion and celery until the vegetables are very soft but not brown. While they are cooking, heat the milk to a simmer.

Add the 6 Tbsp. (90 ml) flour to the vegetables and cook over low heat, stirring constantly for 3-4 minutes. Slowly whisk in the hot milk. The mixture will be very thick. Continue stirring until the mixture comes to a boil.

Remove from the heat and beat in the egg yolks one at a time. Beat in the salt, pepper, Tabasco sauce and parsley. Spread onto a large baking sheet and cool completely. Transfer to a bowl and stir in the crab meat. Refrigerate until firm.

Form the mixture into 12 fat, hamburger-shaped cakes. Sprinkle a baking sheet with 1/4 cup (60 ml) of the bread crumbs. Beat the egg with the water in a shallow bowl. Spread the flour and remaining breadcrumbs on separate plates. Coat each cake in flour, then in the egg, then in the breadcrumbs and place on the baking sheet.

Heat 1 inch (2.5 cm) of vegetable oil in a large heavy frying pan over medium-high heat. Without overcrowding, fry the crab cakes until they are golden brown on both sides. Remove and drain on absorbent paper. Keep the cooked crab cakes warm in a 200°F (100°C) oven while frying the rest. Serve immediately.

Stir-Fried Cellophane Noodles with Dungeness Crab and Pork

Smooth, succulent cellophane noodles are the perfect vehicle for sweet, lush Dungeness crab meat. Serve with a stir-fried green vegetable for a quick meal.

Serves 4

4 oz.	cellophane noodles	115 g
2 Tbsp.	vegetable oil	30 ml
4	cloves garlic, minced	4
4	shallots, finely chopped	4
1/4 lb.	ground pork or turkey	115 g
2	eggs	2
1 Tbsp.	fish sauce*	15 ml
1 tsp.	sugar	5 ml
1/2 tsp.	ground black pepper	2.5 ml
1/4 lb.	crab, picked over	115 g
2	green onions, cut into 1-inch (2.5-cm) lengths	2
	cilantro sprigs for garnish	

*Available at Oriental markets and well-stocked supermarkets.

Soak the noodles in hot water for 30 minutes. Drain well and cut into 2-inch (5-cm) lengths. Heat the oil in a wok or large frying pan over high heat. Stir-fry the garlic and shallots until golden. Add the pork or turkey and stir-fry until it is cooked. Add the eggs and scramble until dry. Add the noodles, fish sauce, sugar and pepper. Stir-fry until the noodles soften and become clear. Stir in the crab and green onions. Turn on to a platter and garnish with the cilantro.

Dungeness Crab and Spinach Bread Pudding

This sumptuous pudding with a peppery Dungeness crab filling can be easily made ahead for a special brunch. You don't have to wait until brunch though— it is wonderful at any meal!

Serves 8

1 lb.	Dungeness crab meat	450 g
12 oz.	spinach, large stems removed, washed and drained	350 g
1 cup	finely diced onion	250 ml
2	medium cloves garlic, minced	2
2 Tbsp.	unsalted butter	30 ml
1/2 tsp.	salt	2.5 ml
1/4 tsp.	black pepper	1.2 ml
	a few gratings of nutmeg	
	a pinch of cayenne pepper	
1 Tbsp.	lemon juice	15 ml
1	2-lb. (900-g) loaf of good-quality unsliced white bread	1
6	large eggs	6
2 Tbsp.	Dijon mustard	30 ml
1/2 tsp.	salt	2.5 ml
	a few gratings of nutmeg	
6 cups	homogenized milk	1.5 L
1/2 lb.	aged white cheddar or asiago cheese, grated	225 g
1 Tbsp.	unsalted butter	15 ml

Pick over the crab meat, removing any bits of shell or cartilage. Place in a large bowl.

Place the spinach in a large covered pot over medium-high heat. Cook, stirring occasionally, until the spinach wilts. Drain and place on a plate to cool. When the spinach has cooled, squeeze out the water and chop finely. Add to the crab.

Sauté the onion and garlic in the 2 Tbsp. (30 ml) butter until translucent. Add the salt, pepper, nutmeg, cayenne and lemon juice. Combine with the crab and spinach and mix well.

Trim the crusts from the bread and cut into 1-inch (2.5-cm) slices.

Beat the eggs, mustard, salt and nutmeg together. Beat in the milk.

Generously butter a 9- by 13-inch (22- by 33-cm) baking pan. Fit one layer of bread into the pan, without overlapping the slices. Spread half the grated cheese evenly over the bread. Spread the crab mixture evenly over the cheese, then top with the remaining cheese. Lay the remaining bread over the crab mixture (overlapping the bread in an attractive manner if you wish).

Carefully pour the egg and milk mixture over the pudding, making sure that the top layer of bread is soaked with the egg and milk mixture. (The pudding can be covered and refrigerated overnight at this point. Bring to room temperature before baking.) Let stand for 1 hour.

Preheat the oven to 350°F (180°C). Bake the pudding for 30 minutes. Remove from the oven and spread the 1 Tbsp. (15 ml) of butter over the top. Return to the oven and bake for 30 minutes longer. Let rest for 15 minutes before serving.

Dungeness Crab Curry

For me, this recipe evokes a time when a wonderful, loving friendship was born. I was doing a menu-tasting for the staff of a restaurant where I was working. When this dish was sampled, I heard particularly happy eating noises at one table. When I cleared the plates, my friend-to-be looked straight at me and said, "I sure would like to have dinner with you." I was startled but intrigued.

To make a long story short, we had many dinners and coffees and even a few "quarter-pounders." It was Paul who kept me inspired during the writing of this book by enticing me out for late-afternoon lattes. He has since moved away, and making this dish is a way of invoking his presence. So, if the recipe seems a bit daunting, take a deep breath, close your eyes and imagine all the happiness it could create for you.

Serves 2 as a main course or 4 as part of a meal

2	live Dungeness crabs, about 1 1/2 lbs. (675 g) each	2
2 Tbsp.	whole coriander seeds	30 ml
1 tsp.	whole black peppercorns	5 ml
2 Tbsp.	bright red, sweet paprika	30 ml
1/2-1 tsp.	cayenne pepper	2.5-5 ml
1/2 tsp.	turmeric	2.5 ml
4 Tbsp.	vegetable oil	60 ml
1 tsp.	black mustard seeds	5 ml
1	medium onion, peeled and sliced into thin half-moons	1
5	cloves garlic, cut into thin slivers	5
2 cups	water	500 ml
2	14-oz. (398-ml) cans coconut milk	2
	salt to taste	

Bring a large pot of water to a boil. Drop in the crabs and cook until they stop moving, about 3-4 minutes. Remove the crabs from the pot and cool. When they are cool enough to handle, pull off and discard the top shell. Scrape the insides clean with a small spoon. Remove the spongy lungs on both sides of the body. With a heavy knife, cut the crabs in quarters and crack the claws. Set aside.

Heat a small frying pan over medium heat. Roast the coriander seeds and peppercorns, stirring constantly, for 1 minute, then grind finely in a spice mill or coffee grinder. Place in a bowl and add the paprika, cayenne and turmeric. Set aside.

Heat the oil over medium heat in a frying pan or pot that will be able to accommodate the crab pieces. Fry the black mustard seeds until they pop. Add the onions and garlic and cook until lightly browned. Stir in the spice mixture and the water. Bring to a boil, then simmer until the mixture is reduced by half. Add the coconut milk and bring to a boil. Season with salt and add the crab. Cook for 5 minutes, turning the pieces over to ensure even cooking. Remove from the heat and serve.

Steamed Manila Clams with Gazpacho Vinaigrette

Another of Andrew's ideas and a perfect summer preparation for clams. Serve with more garlic-rubbed bread to mop up the savory juices.

Serves 4

2 lbs.	fresh Manila clams	900 g
4	1/2-inch-thick (1-cm) slices good sturdy bread	4
1	clove garlic, peeled	1
2 Tbsp.	olive oil	30 ml
1 recipe	Gazpacho Vinaigrette, page 39	1 recipe
	sprigs of cilantro for garnish	

Scrub the clams thoroughly, rinse and drain.

Toast or grill the bread, rub it with the garlic clove and drizzle with the olive oil.

Place the clams and a small amount of water in a heavy pot with a tight-fitting lid. Steam the clams until they open.

Divide the vinaigrette among 4 large bowls, reserving about 1/2 cup (125 ml) as garnish. Place a piece of the garlic-rubbed bread in the middle of each bowl and evenly distribute the clams and their juice among the bowls. Drizzle with the reserved vinaigrette and garnish with the cilantro. Serve immediately.

Steamed Manila Clams with Charred Garlic and Leeks

Rather than tasting burnt, the garlic becomes sweet and smoky. Serve with piles of crusty bread to savor every bit of the briny goodness.

Serves 4

12	cloves garlic, peeled and cut in half	12
1	large leek, white and light green part only, julienned	1
1/2 cup	white wine	125 ml
1 tsp.	cracked black pepper	5 ml
2 lbs.	Manila clams, scrubbed clean	900 g
2 Tbsp.	unsalted butter (optional)	30 ml

Heat a heavy frying pan over medium heat. Cook the garlic, cut side down, until it has blackened.

Place the garlic, leek, white wine, pepper and clams in a heavy pot with a tight-fitting lid. Cook over high heat, shaking the pot occasionally, until the clams open. Swirl in the butter if desired and serve in heated soup bowls.

Grilled Calamari with Fennel and Red Pepper Vinaigrette

If you have never had grilled calamari, this dish will be a revelation. Or, instead of using the fennel dressing, try the Smoked Tomato Vinaigrette, page 40, sprinkled with 3 Tbsp. (45 ml) chopped parsley, 1 tsp. (5 ml) minced garlic and the zest of a lemon.

Roasting Peppers

On a gas stove or barbecue, place the peppers directly on the burners or grill and turn the heat to high. Turn the peppers with tongs as each side is blackened. When the peppers are blackened on all sides, place in a plastic bag until the peppers are cool enough to handle. Slip off the skins and remove the stems and seeds from the peppers. Place in a sieve to drain until ready to use, or for up to 1 hour.

In an oven broiler, broil the peppers on a baking sheet as close to the heat source as possible. Turn the peppers with tongs as each side is blackened and finish as above.

Choosing and Cooking Calamari

There are a few things to keep in mind when cooking calamari. If you are buying thawed calamari from a seafood case, it should look pearly white with flecks of brown or black on the skin. Calamari that is turning purple is past its prime and should be avoided. The best way to obtain perfectly fresh calamari is to buy it frozen. It is usually sold in 2-, 3- or 5-pound (900-, 1300- or 2200-g) blocks at fish stores or large supermarkets. Thaw it under cold running water or for 2 days in the fridge. The advantage of thawing it under water is that you can take off as much as you need as it thaws. Wrap the still-frozen portion tightly and keep it in the freezer.

The second thing of importance is the cooking of calamari. It has to be cooked briefly or *long and slowly to remain tender. Anything in between will produce chewy, chewy calamari—not a pleasant thing to eat at all.*

Serves 6

1 Tbsp.	red wine vinegar	15 ml
1/4 tsp.	salt	1.2 ml
1/2 cup	olive oil	125 ml
1	red pepper, roasted, peeled and seeded, and diced	1
1 1/2 tsp.	fennel or anise seeds	7.5 ml
2 Tbsp.	finely chopped parsley	30 ml
1	medium clove garlic, minced	1
	finely chopped zest of 1 lemon	
2 lbs.	small calamari, cleaned	900 g
	salt and pepper to taste	
1 Tbsp.	olive oil	15 ml

To make the vinaigrette, stir the vinegar and salt together. Slowly beat in the olive oil. Add the red pepper. In a small, heavy frying pan over medium heat, toast the fennel or anise seeds, shaking the pan constantly until the seeds turn a shade darker. Add to the vinaigrette.

Combine the parsley, garlic and lemon zest in a small bowl and set aside.

Preheat the barbecue on its highest setting. Toss the calamari with the salt, pepper and olive oil and place them on the grill. When they are marked by the grill, turn them over and mark on the other side. Place the calamari on a heated platter, pour the vinaigrette over them and sprinkle with the parsley mixture. Serve immediately.

Pan-Seared Skate with Beef Stock

If I had to choose my favorite fish dish, I would be torn between this and Alaskan Black Cod Ossobuco, page 78. This is simple, elegant and outrageously delicious. Serve with Horseradish Mashed Potatoes, page 126.

Serves 4

4	6-oz. (180-g) pieces of skate	4
	salt and pepper to taste	
1/2 cup	all-purpose flour	125 ml
1/2 tsp.	paprika	2.5 ml
2 Tbsp.	vegetable oil	30 ml
4 cups	Beef Stock, page 199	1 L

Preheat the oven to 400°F (200°C). Wash the skate and pat dry. Season with salt and pepper. Mix the flour and paprika together on a plate.

Heat the oil over medium heat in a large heavy skillet. Dip both sides of the skate into the flour and shake off the excess. Fry on both sides until golden brown. Transfer to a baking pan and bake for 15 minutes until the flesh turns opaque in the middle.

While the skate is baking, pour off all the oil from the frying pan. Add the beef stock and bring to a boil, scraping up any bits clinging to the frying pan. Reduce the beef stock by half. Season with salt and pepper. Remove from the heat and keep warm.

Place the skate on heated plates. Pour the beef stock over it and serve immediately.

Pan-Seared Skate with Burnt Orange and Wasabi Glaze

The burnt orange and wasabi glaze is a charming companion to halibut, prawns and salmon as well.

Serves 6

6	5- to 6-oz. (150- to 180-g) pieces of skate	6
	salt and pepper to taste	
1 Tbsp.	vegetable oil	15 ml

Preheat the oven to 350°F (180°C). Season the skate with salt and pepper. Heat the oil in a heavy frying pan or two over medium-high heat and cook the skate until it is lightly browned on both sides. Bake in the oven for 15 minutes, until opaque throughout. Place on heated plates or a platter. Spoon the sauce over the skate and serve immediately.

Burnt Orange and Wasabi Glaze

3/4 cup	granulated sugar	185 ml
1/4 cup	water	60 ml
1/2 cup	red wine	125 ml
1/4 tsp.	salt	1.2 ml
1	orange, juice and grated rind	1
1 Tbsp.	prepared wasabi,* or to taste	15 ml
2-4 Tbsp.	unsalted butter	30-60 ml
2	green onions, julienned	2

*Available at Japanese markets and well-stocked supermarkets.

To make the glaze, combine the sugar and water in a small, heavy saucepan. Cook over high heat without stirring until the sugar turns a dark mahogany brown. Watch the caramel carefully. You will see the bubbles rise more rapidly and become looser and less viscous.

Remove from the heat, stand back and immediately pour the red wine through a sieve that covers the pot completely. The caramel will splutter furiously. The sieve will protect you from burns.

When the spluttering stops, transfer the caramel to a bowl and add the salt. Cool completely and add the orange juice and rind. (The glaze may be made to this point up to 1 week in advance.) Cover and refrigerate.

Just before serving, bring the glaze to a boil. Whisk in the wasabi. Remove from the heat and whisk in the butter, 1 Tbsp. (15 ml) at a time. Add the green onions.

Oven-Roasted Halibut with Lemon Balm Butter

Lemon balm is a fragrant perennial herb that requires no care. It can be added to a salad for a lemony lift, or brewed into herbal tea. This sauce complements salmon or sole.

Serves 4

2 Tbsp.	apple cider vinegar	30 ml
1 Tbsp.	water	15 ml
1/4 tsp.	salt	1.2 ml
1 Tbsp.	finely chopped shallots	15 ml
8 oz.	cold unsalted butter cut into 1/2-inch (1-cm) cubes	225 g
2 Tbsp.	coarsely chopped lemon balm leaves	30 ml
4	6-oz. (180-g) halibut filets	4
	salt and pepper to taste	

To make the lemon balm butter, combine the vinegar, water, salt and shallots in a small saucepan. Bring to a boil and reduce the mixture to 1 Tbsp. (15 ml). Remove from the heat and turn the heat to low.

Whisk in the butter 2 cubes at a time, waiting until the pieces have been incorporated before adding more. Control the melting point by moving the pot on and off the heat. If the mixture becomes too hot, the butter will separate. When all the butter has been incorporated, stir in the lemon balm. Set aside.

Preheat the oven to 400°F (200°C). Lightly salt and pepper the halibut filets and place them skin-side down in a baking pan. Bake for 10-15 minutes until the flesh turns opaque in the middle.

Place the halibut on a heated platter or plates. Pour the lemon balm butter over the filets and serve immediately.

Pan-Roasted Halibut with Lentil and Tomato Vinaigrette

Fresh halibut has a limited run, confined to the summer months. To fully savor its wonderful texture and sweet flavor, I like to pair it with sauces that won't interfere with that experience.

Serves 6

1 cup	small brown lentils	250 ml
1	small onion studded with a clove	1
1	1-inch (2.5-cm) piece cinnamon stick	1
1	2-inch (5-cm) piece carrot, peeled	1
1	2-inch (5-cm) piece celery	1
1	medium clove garlic, minced	1
1/2 tsp.	salt	2.5 ml
2 Tbsp.	balsamic vinegar	30 ml
2 Tbsp.	olive oil	30 ml
2 Tbsp.	vegetable oil	30 ml
	pepper to taste	
6	5- to 6-oz. (150- to 180-g) skinless halibut filets	6
	salt and pepper to taste	
1 Tbsp.	vegetable oil	15 ml
2	medium, ripe tomatoes, seeded and finely diced	2
1 Tbsp.	finely chopped parsley	15 ml

Wash and drain the lentils, place them in a pot and cover with 4 inches (10 cm) of water. Bring to a boil over high heat, reduce to a simmer and skim off any foam that rises to the top. Add the onion, cinnamon stick, carrot and celery. Simmer until the lentils are tender but not mushy. Drain and discard the vegetables and cinnamon stick.

While waiting for the lentils to cook, mash the garlic to a paste with the salt. Whisk in the balsamic vinegar, then slowly beat in the olive and vegetable oils. Season with pepper. Combine the warm lentils with the vinaigrette and stir well to coat.

Preheat the oven to 350°F (180°C). Sprinkle the halibut filets with salt and pepper. Heat the 1 Tbsp. (15 ml) oil on medium-high heat in a heavy, ovenproof frying pan. Fry the halibut skin-side up until golden brown. Flip the filets over and bake in the oven for 10 minutes.

Mix the tomatoes and parsley into the lentils and spoon onto 6 heated plates. Place the halibut on top of the lentils and serve immediately.

Crispy Red Snapper with Sweet and Sour Cucumber-Beer Relish

Try the cucumber and beer relish with freshly shucked oysters.

Serves 4-6

2 lbs.	red snapper filets	900 g
1/4 cup	egg whites	60 ml
1/4 tsp.	salt	1.2 ml
1/8 tsp.	black pepper	.5 ml
1 Tbsp.	Dijon mustard	15 ml
	a few drops of Tabasco sauce	
1/4 cup	cornstarch	60 ml
6 cups	soft white bread crumbs (see page 50)	1.5 L
	vegetable oil for frying	

Cut the snapper filets in half if they are large. Beat the egg whites, salt, pepper, mustard, Tabasco and cornstarch together. Dip the snapper into the cornstarch mixture then dredge with the bread crumbs, patting them on firmly with your hands.

Heat 1/2 inch (1 cm) of vegetable oil in a large heavy frying pan over medium heat. Fry the snapper filets until golden brown on both sides and cooked through. Serve immediately, with the relish on the side.

Sweet and Sour Cucumber-Beer Relish

1 cup	white vinegar	250 ml
10 Tbsp.	granulated sugar	150 ml
1	English cucumber, sliced paper thin	1
2 tsp.	salt	10 ml
1/2 cup	beer	125 ml
4	shallots, thinly sliced	4

Combine the vinegar and sugar in a noncorrodible saucepan. Bring to a boil and boil hard for 5 minutes. Remove from the heat and cool.

Toss the sliced cucumbers with the salt. Place in a sieve and weight with a bowl that fits into the sieve. Allow the cucumbers to drain for an hour. Gently squeeze the cucumbers with your hands to remove any water. Place in a bowl. (The relish may be made to this point a few hours in advance. Pour off any liquid that has accumulated around the cucumbers before proceeding.)

Just before serving, mix the beer with the vinegar syrup. Pour over the cucumbers and mix gently. Scatter the shallots on top.

Halibut Cheeks Roasted on Potato Crisps

Halibut season is the time for halibut cheeks. For me, the cheeks are the most satisfying part of the whole fish. This recipe shows them off beautifully.

You can use almost any firm-fleshed white fish for this dish, such as cod, sea bass or red snapper. Just make sure the fish is about 1 inch (2.5 cm) thick.

Serves 4

1 1/2 lbs.	red-skinned potatoes	675 g
5 Tbsp.	olive oil	75 ml
6	garlic cloves, cut in half	6
1/2 tsp.	salt	2.5 ml
1/4 tsp.	pepper	1.2 ml
8	3- to 4-oz. (90- to 120-g) halibut cheeks, or 5- to 6-oz. (150- to 180-g) halibut filets	8
	salt and pepper to taste	
1	plum tomato, peeled, seeded and diced	1
2	bay leaves, crumbled	2
4	sprigs fresh thyme	4
1/4 tsp.	fennel seeds	1.2 ml

Preheat the oven to 425°F (220°C). Slice the potatoes very thinly, as if you were making potato chips. Wash the slices, drain them well and dry with a tea towel. In a large bowl, combine the potatoes, 4 Tbsp. (60 ml) of the olive oil, and the garlic, salt and pepper. Toss well and spread evenly in a 9- by 13-inch (22- by 33-cm) baking pan (do not use a glass pan). Bake for 20 minutes, turning every 5 minutes.

Season the fish with salt, pepper and the remaining tablespoon (15 ml) of olive oil. Scatter the tomato, bay leaves, thyme and fennel seeds over the potatoes and place the fish on top. Bake for 5 minutes if using the cheeks, 10 minutes if using filets.

Remove from the oven and preheat the broiler. Return to the oven and broil until the potatoes around the edge of the dish turn crispy, about 5 minutes. Remove from the oven and serve immediately.

Arctic Char Filets with Tomato and Nasturtium Relish

Nasturtiums are easily grown from seed and thrive in poor soil. Both the leaves and flowers are edible and add a peppery punch to dishes when served raw. Salmon or trout may be substituted for Arctic char in this dish.

Salting Tomatoes

Salting tomatoes removes the water that will dilute the flavor when they are used raw, in an uncooked sauce. When the water is removed, the sauce will taste more intensely of tomato.

Serves 6

8	ripe plum tomatoes, peeled, seeded and diced	8
1 tsp.	salt	5 ml
2 tsp.	extra virgin olive oil	10 ml
6	5- to 6-oz. (150- to 180-g) Arctic char	6
	salt and pepper to taste	
2 Tbsp.	finely chopped shallots	30 ml
30	nasturtium flowers, petals removed and reserved	30
1 tsp.	freshly ground black pepper	5 ml
	a few drops of lemon juice if the tomatoes are very sweet	

Combine the tomatoes and salt. Place in a sieve and drain for 1/2 hour. Set aside.

Preheat the oven to 350°F (180°C). Spread the olive oil in a baking dish large enough to hold the fish in a single layer. Sprinkle with salt and pepper and scatter with the shallots. Bake the filets until they are firm, about 10 minutes. Place the fish on a serving platter, and reserve the juices.

Combine the tomatoes with the fish juices, nasturtium petals, pepper and lemon juice, if desired. Taste and adjust seasoning. Spoon over the fish filets and serve.

Edible Flowers

Flowers can add flavor as well as eye appeal.

Borage: *Pale blue flowers with a pointed black center and marked cucumber flavor. Use where a hint of cucumber is wanted.*

Arugula: *White flowers with brown stripes, and a more intense flavor than the leaves but without any bitterness.*

Sage: *The subtle fragrance of sage with an intoxicating honey aroma. Use in the same way as lavender flowers.*

Lavender: *Crush and add a small amount to chicken and fish marinades, or creamy desserts such as crème brulée or pastry creams.*

Bok choy, sui choy, broccoli: *If you grow these vegetables and they have bolted, try eating the bright yellow flowers. Pungently flavored, they are an interesting addition to salads.*

Alaskan Black Cod Ossobuco

When I first tasted black cod, I became an instant convert. Also known as sablefish, it is a richly textured fish with a suave, buttery flavor. It reminded us so much of veal that my husband, Steven, suggested serving it with the traditional sauce and garnish for ossobuco. It worked perfectly but was elevated to stardom when accompanied by Saffron Risotto, page138.

Serves 6

4 Tbsp.	unsalted butter	60 ml
1 cup	finely chopped onion	250 ml
2/3 cup	finely chopped carrot	160 ml
2/3 cup	finely chopped celery	160 ml
1 Tbsp.	finely chopped parsley	15 ml
2	medium cloves garlic, minced	2
2	strips lemon peel, peeled from a lemon with a vegetable peeler	2
2	bay leaves	2
1 1/2 cups	canned tomatoes, with juice, puréed and sieved to remove the seeds	375 ml
1 cup	white wine	250 ml
3 cups	beef or chicken stock	750 ml
	salt and pepper to taste	
2 Tbsp.	finely chopped parsley	30 ml
2 tsp.	lemon peel, grated	10 ml
1/2 tsp.	garlic, minced	2.5 ml
6	black cod steaks, 1 1/2 inches (4 cm) thick	6
	salt and pepper to taste	
2 Tbsp.	vegetable oil	30 ml
1/2 cup	all-purpose flour	125 ml

To make the sauce, melt the butter over medium heat in a large saucepan. Add the onion, carrot, celery and parsley and sauté until the vegetables are soft but not browned, 8-10 minutes.

Add the garlic, lemon peel, bay leaves, tomatoes, wine and stock. Bring to a boil, then reduce to a simmer. Cook for approximately 1 1/2 hours, stirring occasionally until reduced by two-thirds and thickened. Season with salt and pepper and remove from the heat. (The sauce may be prepared up to 2 days in advance. When cool, cover and refrigerate.)

When you are ready to finish the dish, combine the parsley, lemon peel and garlic in a small bowl and set aside.

Preheat the oven to 350°F (180°C). Salt and pepper the cod steaks. Heat the vegetable oil in a large, heavy frying pan over medium heat. Dip the steaks into the flour and shake off the excess. Fry until golden brown on both sides.

Remove from the pan and place in a single layer in a baking dish. Heat the sauce to a boil and pour over the cod. Bake for 15 minutes. Sprinkle the parsley, garlic and lemon garnish over the cod and serve immediately.

Pancetta-Wrapped Cod with Smoked Tomato Vinaigrette

If you thought cod was a dull fish, this will change your mind. It changed mine. Also try it with the lentil and tomato vinaigrette for halibut, page 74.

Serves 6

6	5- to 6-oz. (150- to 180-g) filets of ling cod or true cod	6
	salt and pepper to taste	
12	thin slices pancetta	12
1 Tbsp.	vegetable oil	15 ml
1 recipe	Smoked Tomato Vinaigrette, page 40	1 recipe

Lightly salt and pepper both sides of the cod. Place the pancetta on one side of the cod.

Preheat the oven to 350°F (180°C). Heat the vegetable oil in a large frying pan over medium heat. Slip in the cod, pancetta side down. Fry until the pancetta is lightly browned. Flip the cod over and fry until the bottom is lightly browned.

Transfer to a baking sheet, pancetta-side up, and bake until the cod just turns opaque, 5-7 minutes. Don't overcook the cod—it turns to cotton if you do.

Serve on warm plates or a platter, drizzled with or surrounded by the vinaigrette.

Smoked Black Cod Poached in Mulled Apple Cider

Smoked black cod is a Pacific Northwest treat that is seldom seen anywhere else. It is smoky and buttery, with luscious, firm meat. Some smoked cod is oversalted and dyed an unnatural fluorescent red, but it is worth your while to seek out natural smoked black cod.

Serves 4

4 cups	nonalcoholic apple cider	1 L
1	4-inch (10-cm) piece cinnamon stick	1
4	whole cloves	4
12	whole black peppercorns	12
1	whole cardamom pod	1
1	bay leaf	1
1/2 tsp	fennel seeds	2.5 ml
4	5- to 6-oz. (150- to 180-g) skinless filets of natural smoked black cod	4

Combine the cider and spices in a noncorrodible frying pan that will snugly accommodate the cod filets. Bring to a boil, cover and simmer gently for 15 minutes. Slip the filets into the pan and poach gently for 10 minutes. Remove from the pan, cover and keep warm.

Rapidly reduce the spiced cider to 2 cups (500 ml). Strain through a sieve (or you may opt for the natural look and leave the spices in). Place the fish on heated plates and pour the reduced cider over the fish. Serve immediately.

Pan-Roasted Flounder with Garlic and Chilies

Flatfish are great fish to serve whole. They look impressive on the plate and the meat lifts cleanly off the bones.

Serves 4

4	flounders, 1 lb. (450 g) each, gutted, skinned and head removed	4
	salt and pepper to taste	
1/2 cup	all-purpose flour	125 ml
2 tsp.	paprika	10 ml
2 Tbsp.	olive oil	30 ml
8	whole dried hot chili peppers	8
4	medium cloves garlic, thinly sliced	4
	lemon wedges	

Preheat the oven to 350°F (180°C). Salt and pepper the flounders. Mix the flour and paprika together on a plate.

Heat the olive oil in a large, heavy, ovenproof frying pan over medium heat. If you do not have a frying pan large enough to hold the fish in a single layer, use two frying pans, dividing the ingredients in half and increasing the olive oil to 4 Tbsp. (60 ml).

Fry the chilies in the oil until they swell, then add the garlic. When it starts to sizzle, quickly coat the flounder with the flour and fry until golden brown on both sides. Place the pan in the oven and bake for 10 minutes. Remove from the oven and serve immediately with the lemon wedges. Warn your guests to avoid the chilies unless they can take the heat.

Grilled Steelhead Trout Filets with Lavender Butter

Steelhead trout are a seasonal treat that make their appearance in late fall. They are large ocean-going trout that are similar to salmon in appearance. Their flesh is pink and a sweet cross between salmon and trout.

Serves 6

3 Tbsp.	apple cider vinegar	45 ml
1/4 tsp.	salt	1.2 ml
1 Tbsp.	finely chopped shallots	15 ml
8 oz.	cold, unsalted butter, cut into 1/2-inch (1-cm) cubes	225 g
1 Tbsp.	finely chopped lavender leaves	15 ml
6	6-oz. (180-g) steelhead trout or salmon filets	6
	salt and pepper to taste	
	flour for dredging	
	vegetable oil	

To make the sauce, combine the vinegar, salt and shallots in a small, noncorrodible saucepan. Cook over high heat until the mixture is reduced by half. Reduce the heat to very low and remove the pan from the heat. Whisk in the butter cubes one at a time, making sure each cube is absorbed before adding another. Do not let the sauce boil or it will separate. Regulate the heat by moving the pan on and off the burner. The sauce will gradually thicken to the consistency of heavy cream. Remove from the heat. Stir in the lavender leaves.

Preheat the barbecue to high. Salt and pepper the fish, dip both sides in the flour, then into the oil. Grill 2-3 minutes on each side until done to your liking. Remove from the grill and place on heated plates or a large platter. Pour the sauce over the filets and serve immediately.

Salmon Pastrami

This tastes and smells just like pastrami, but with a salmon flavor. Serve it as an appetizer, on top of scrambled eggs or as the obvious—a sandwich on light sour rye bread.

Makes 1 1/2 lbs. (675 g)

10	medium cloves garlic, peeled and sliced	10
1	celery stalk, chopped	1
1/3 cup	salt	80 ml
1/4 cup	granulated sugar	60 ml
2 Tbsp.	black peppercorns	30 ml
1 Tbsp.	coriander seeds	15 ml
1 Tbsp.	yellow mustard seeds	15 ml
10	whole cloves	10
6	bay leaves	6
1	whole dried chili pepper	1
1/8 tsp.	cinnamon	.5 ml
2 tsp.	paprika	10 ml
2 Tbsp.	Worcestershire sauce	30 ml
2 tsp.	liquid smoke	10 ml
1	boneless salmon filet with the skin on, 1 3/4-2 lbs. (800-900 g)	1

Combine the garlic, celery stalk, salt and sugar in the work bowl of a food processor. Coarsely grind the peppercorns, coriander seeds, mustard seeds, cloves, bay leaf and chili pepper. Add to the salt mixture with the cinnamon, paprika, Worcestershire sauce and liquid smoke. Process until the garlic is finely chopped and the whole mixture is evenly wet.

Prick the skin side of the salmon filet about 40 times with a pin. Spread a third of the mixture over the skin and the remaining mixture on the top of the filet. Wrap securely with plastic wrap and place on a tray. Cover with another tray and weight down with tinned goods or bottles of water. Refrigerate for 4 days.

Unwrap the salmon and scrape off the marinade. Wash under cold water and pat dry. To serve, slice the salmon extremely thinly on the diagonal, starting at the tail end.

Poached Salmon with Ginger and Black Bean Vinaigrette

Salmon looks stunning surrounded by this black bean vinaigrette and it can be served cold in the summer. Also try the vinaigrette with poached or grilled prawns; it is an exceptional combination.

Serves 4

1 cup	white wine	250 ml
4	1/4-inch (.5-cm) slices ginger, lightly crushed	4
1	star anise	1
1 Tbsp.	sugar	15 ml
2	green onions, lightly crushed	2
2 tsp.	salt	10 ml
1	whole dried chili pepper	1
4 cups	water	1 L
4	6-oz. (180-g) salmon filets	4

Combine all ingredients except the salmon in a noncorrodible pan that will fit the salmon snugly. Bring to a boil, then simmer for 15 minutes, partially covered with a lid.

Slip the salmon filets into the liquid and poach gently for 10 minutes. Remove from the liquid. If you wish to serve the salmon cold, cool to room temperature, then cover and refrigerate. (The salmon may be prepared 1 day in advance.) To serve hot, transfer to heated plates or a platter. Spoon the vinaigrette around the salmon and serve immediately.

Ginger and Black Bean Vinaigrette

2	medium cloves garlic, minced	2
1 Tbsp.	fresh ginger, minced	15 ml
1/2 cup	pickled ginger (see page 193, or buy)	125 ml
3 Tbsp.	pickled ginger juice	45 ml
2 Tbsp.	apple cider vinegar	30 ml
3/4 tsp.	salt	4 ml
3 Tbsp.	sugar	45 ml
1/4 cup	fermented black beans*	60 ml
3/4 cup	vegetable oil	185 ml

*Available at Oriental markets and well-stocked supermarkets.

Make the vinaigrette at least a day before using. Combine all ingredients except the vegetable oil in the work bowl of a food processor or blender. Pulse until very finely chopped. With the motor running, add the vegetable oil in a slow steady stream and process until well blended. Cover and refrigerate. (The vinaigrette will keep for up to a week in the refrigerator. Bring it to room temperature before serving.)

Salmon Baked in Parchment with Hearts and Ribbons

We make this for Valentine's Day. When the package is opened at the table it always elicits sighs of delight. Change the hearts to stars for another occasion, such as New Year's Eve.

Serves 4

8	carrot ribbons and hearts	8
8	daikon radish ribbons and hearts	8
8	butternut squash ribbons and hearts	8
4	16- by 20-inch (40- by 50-cm) pieces of parchment paper	4
4	5- to 6-oz. (150- to 180-g) salmon filets or steaks	4
	salt and pepper to taste	
2 Tbsp.	coarsely chopped dill	30 ml
2	green onions, julienned	2
4 Tbsp.	white wine	60 ml
2 Tbsp.	unsalted butter	30 ml
	vegetable oil	

To make hearts, cut 1/4-inch (.5-cm) slices from each of the vegetables. Using a small, heart-shaped cookie cutter, cut hearts out of the vegetable slices. To make the ribbons, pare long strips of each of the vegetables with a vegetable peeler.

Fold the parchment paper in half lengthwise. Cut a half-heart shape out of the parchment, starting at the fold. When opened up you will have a heart-shaped piece of parchment paper. Stack the vegetable ribbons and cut into a long fine julienne. Preheat the oven to 425°F (220°C).

Season the salmon with salt and pepper. Place a piece on one side of each parchment heart.

Toss the vegetables, dill and green onions together and scatter over the salmon. Add 1 Tbsp. (15 ml) white wine and 1/2 Tbsp. (7.5 ml) butter to each of the salmon pieces.

Fold the other side of the heart over the salmon. Fold and press the edges tightly inward to enclose the salmon. Brush the outside with vegetable oil. Place on a baking sheet and bake for 15 minutes. Remove from the oven and place on preheated plates. Cut an X with a pair of scissors in the top of each package for easy opening at the table. Serve immediately.

Salmon Baked in Corn Husks with Corn and Zucchini Sauté

This is very easy and always a show-stopper.

Serves 4

4	whole ears of corn	4
4	5- to 6-oz. (150- to 180-g) skinless salmon filets	4
	salt and pepper to taste	
4 Tbsp.	unsalted butter	60 ml
1 cup	diced red onion	250 ml
1 cup	diced zucchini	250 ml

Carefully peel back the corn husks and snap the cob at the bottom, leaving the husks attached to the stem. Discard the silk and any blemished leaves. Set the husks aside.

Cut 2 cups (500 ml) of kernels from the corn and set aside.

Preheat the oven to 350°F (180°C). Lightly salt and pepper the salmon filets. Separate the leaves of each corn husk and tuck a salmon filet into the middle, enclosing it within the husk. Don't try to make it look neat. Tear 4 strips from the discarded leaves and use them to tie the opened end of the husk. Place on a baking sheet and bake for 20 minutes.

While the salmon is baking, melt the butter in a saucepan over medium heat and sauté the red onions until they are translucent. Sauté the zucchini until it just begins to soften. Add the corn and continue to cook until it is heated through.

Place the salmon on heated plates or a platter. Fold back the top of the corn husks and tuck them under the stem. Spoon the corn sauté over the salmon. Serve immediately to a chorus of "oohs" and "aahs." Take a bow.

Salmon Cooked on One Side with Raisin Vinaigrette

This unusual way of cooking salmon keeps it moist and succulent. If you have never had a medium-rare piece of salmon, you are missing out on one of the great eating pleasures of all time. The sweet, sour and salty elements of the vinaigrette are the perfect complement to the salmon.

Serves 4

2 Tbsp.	golden raisins	30 ml
4 Tbsp.	cider vinegar	60 ml
2 Tbsp.	water	30 ml
6 Tbsp.	thinly sliced shallots	90 ml
3 Tbsp.	olive oil	45 ml
6	pitted green olives, thinly sliced	6
2 Tbsp.	drained capers	30 ml
4-5 oz.	salmon filets, with the skin on	120-150 g
1/2 tsp.	salt	2.5 ml

To make the sauce, put the raisins, vinegar and water in a small saucepan and bring to a boil over high heat. Cover tightly and set aside.

Sauté the shallots in the olive oil until golden brown. Remove from the heat and add the raisins, olives and capers. Set aside in a warm place.

To cook the salmon, heat a heavy cast-iron or another sturdy pan over low heat for 5 minutes. Place the salmon skin-side down in the pan, sprinkle with salt and cook for 20 minutes without turning. The salmon will remain moist and pink in the middle and the skin will become crisp.

Place the salmon on warmed plates and spoon the sauce over it.

Poultry

Braised Chicken with Dried Apples and Prunes

Serve this winter chicken dish with egg noodles or Mashed Sweet Potatoes with Blue Cheese, page 124.

Serves 4

1	3-lb. (1.3-kg) chicken cut into serving pieces	1
1/2 cup	flour	125 ml
2 Tbsp.	vegetable oil	30 ml
2	cloves garlic, minced	2
1 cup	onion, cut into 1-inch (2.5-cm) dice	250 ml
6 cups	chicken stock or water	1.5 L
1 cup	red wine	250 ml
1/2 tsp.	salt	2.5 ml
2	cloves	2
1/8 tsp.	caraway seeds	.5 ml
1	1-inch (2.5-cm) piece cinnamon stick	1
1	bay leaf	1
16	pitted prunes	16
2/3 cup	dried apple slices	160 ml

Dredge each piece of chicken in the flour. Heat the vegetable oil over medium heat in a wide heavy frying pan. Sauté the chicken on both sides until golden brown and transfer to a plate.

Add the garlic and onion to the pan and sauté until the onions are translucent. Return the chicken to the pan and add the stock or water and red wine. If the liquid does not cover the chicken, add enough stock or water to cover the chicken by 2 inches (5 cm). Bring to a boil, skimming off any foam that rises to the top. Add the remaining ingredients and reduce to a simmer. Cover and simmer for 40 minutes or until the chicken is tender.

Transfer the chicken from the pan to a plate and cover. Bring the liquid to a boil and reduce until it becomes syrupy. Return the chicken to the pan, turn down to a simmer and heat the chicken through.

Pepper and Cilantro Marinated Chicken (a.k.a. Thai Barbecue Chicken)

This is a "knock 'em dead" recipe. Its popularity is due to it being a) extremely tasty, b) easy to make, and c) a lot of fun to eat.

Serves 6

1 bunch	fresh cilantro, washed and dried	1 bunch
1 tsp.	black pepper	5 ml
3 Tbsp.	fish sauce or soya sauce	45 ml
2	cloves garlic, minced	2
6	boneless chicken breasts, skin left on	6
1 head	leaf lettuce, washed and dried	1 head
1/2	English cucumber, sliced	1/2
1 bunch	mint, washed and dried	1 bunch
1 recipe	Sweet and Sour Dipping Sauce, page 198	1 recipe

Divide the bunch of cilantro in half and set one half aside. Place the remaining cilantro, pepper, fish sauce and garlic in a food processor or blender and pulse until the cilantro is finely chopped. Alternatively, finely chop the cilantro and combine with the pepper, fish sauce and garlic. Pour over the chicken and marinate for at least 2 hours or overnight.

When you are ready to cook the chicken, preheat the broiler or barbecue. Cook the chicken until the skin is crispy and the meat is cooked all the way through, 4-5 minutes per side. Arrange the lettuce, cucumber, mint and the half-bunch of cilantro attractively on a platter. Place the dipping sauce in 6 individual bowls. Cut the chicken into 1-inch (2.5-cm) pieces and serve with the vegetable platter and dipping sauce.

To eat the chicken, take a piece of lettuce and tear it in half. Place a slice of cucumber, a bit of mint, cilantro and piece of chicken on the lettuce. Roll the lettuce up, dip it into the sauce and enjoy.

Chicken Breasts with Tomatoes, Basil and Roasted Garlic

Fast and easy. Serve with a loaf of good bread to mop up the juice. A nice variation is to add 1/2 cup (125 ml) of crumbled feta when you add the basil.

Serves 4

4	boneless, skinless chicken breasts	4
	salt and pepper	
1 Tbsp.	olive oil	15 ml
2	medium, ripe tomatoes, cut into 8 wedges each	2
12	cloves roasted garlic, page 196	12
1/2 cup	fresh basil leaves	125 ml
	salt and pepper to taste	

Salt and pepper the chicken breasts. Heat the olive oil in a large frying pan over medium heat. Cook the chicken on both sides until lightly browned. Add the tomatoes and garlic to the pan. Cover, turn the heat to low and simmer for 5 minutes. Add the basil and cook until it wilts. Season with salt and pepper and serve immediately.

Chicken Breasts Baked with Grapes and Tarragon

If you can beg some from a grape-growing neighbor, line the bottom of the baking dish with grape leaves. They are edible. Serve straight from the dish with wild or white rice.

Serves 4

4	boneless, skinless chicken breasts	4
3/4 cup	red or green seedless grapes, cut in half (muscats are great if you can find them)	185 ml
2 tsp.	honey	10 ml
1	green onion, thinly sliced	1
1/4 tsp.	salt	1.2 ml
1 tsp.	chopped fresh tarragon leaves	5 ml
1 tsp.	apple cider vinegar	5 ml

Preheat the oven to 350°F (180°C). Place the chicken breasts in a single layer in a lightly buttered baking dish. Mix the remaining ingredients together and scatter over the chicken. Cover with a lid or tin foil and bake for 10 minutes. Remove the cover and bake 10 minutes longer.

Casseroled Chicken with Bacon, Cream and Thyme

This recipe, inspired by former coworker Marnie, has a cozy, old-fashioned taste and appearance. If you have a cast-iron pan, use it for cooking and serving the chicken in.

Serves 4

4	boneless 6-oz. (180-g) chicken breasts, with skin	4
8	slices bacon	8
8	small sprigs fresh thyme	8
1 Tbsp.	vegetable oil	15 ml
1	clove garlic, minced	1
1/2 cup	chicken stock or water	125 ml
1 cup	35% cream	250 ml
	salt and pepper to taste	

Wrap two pieces of bacon around each piece of chicken to form an X in the middle of each breast. Tuck a piece of thyme behind each X.

Preheat the oven to 350°F (180°C). Heat the vegetable oil over medium heat in a large, heavy frying pan that can go into the oven. Add the chicken breasts, bacon side down, and cook until the bacon is browned. Turn the chicken over and cook on the other side until browned. Remove the chicken to a plate and discard the fat. Add the garlic, chicken stock or water, and cream. Season with salt and pepper. Bring to a boil and return the chicken to the pan.

Place in the oven and bake for 20 minutes. If the cream seems too thin at the end of cooking, return the pan to the stove and boil over high heat until the cream is lightly thickened. Serve immediately.

Chicken and Leek Stew

My husband Steven has a great love of leeks. I have to confess that I do not share his passion for them in general, but I very much enjoy the silky texture and shyly sweet flavor in this stew.

Serves 3-4

1	chicken, approximately 2 1/4 lbs. (1 kg)	1
5 cups	water or chicken stock	1.2 L
4	large leeks, white and pale green parts only, cut in half lengthwise and cut into 2-inch (5-cm) pieces	4
3	medium carrots, peeled and cut in half lengthwise, then cut into 1-inch (2.5-cm) diagonals	3
2	stalks celery, cut into 2-inch (5-cm) pieces	2
1	bay leaf	1
1 cup	white wine	250 ml
1/2 tsp.	salt	2.5 ml
	salt and pepper to taste	
2	egg yolks (optional)	2
2 Tbsp.	lemon juice	30 ml
1 tsp.	minced lemon zest	5 ml
1 tsp.	fresh tarragon, or 1 Tbsp. (15 ml) fresh parsley, minced	5 ml

Cut the chicken into 8 serving pieces. Remove the skin and trim off any fat. Place the chicken in a large pot and add enough water or stock to cover the chicken by 1 inch (2.5 cm). Bring to a boil, skimming off any foam that rises to the top. Add the vegetables, bay leaf, white wine, salt and enough additional water or stock to cover the vegetables.

Return to a boil, then reduce to a bare simmer. Cook for 1 hour, skimming off any foam that rises to the top.

Remove the chicken and vegetables from the cooking liquid. Skim off any fat, turn the heat to high and reduce the liquid to 8 cups (2 L).

Return the chicken and vegetables to the cooking liquid. Season to taste with salt and pepper.

Egg Yolk Liaison

An egg yolk liaison is a traditional French technique used as a light thickener that adds a rich creamy texture to soups, stews and sauces. In the evolution of cooking techniques it has almost become obsolete because the leftovers cannot be reheated well. But do try it—it is delicious!

To add an egg yolk liaison to a dish, ensure that the liquid you are adding it to is barely simmering. Beat a few spoonfuls of the hot liquid into the yolks. Remove the pot from the heat, then stir in the yolk mixture. Do not add to boiling liquid or bring to a boil after adding or you will end up with scrambled egg floating around in your dish. Serve immediately.

If you want to use the egg yolks, beat them together with the lemon juice, zest, and tarragon and a few spoonfuls of the cooking liquid. Reheat the stew. Remove the pot from the heat and stir in the egg yolk mixture, shaking the pan gently to distribute the mixture evenly. If you are not using the egg yolks, add the lemon juice, zest and tarragon to the stew. Serve immediately in heated soup plates.

Chicken Breasts Baked with Pears and Pear Brandy

Serve this simple and elegant chicken dish with mashed potatoes and steamed spinach.

Serves 4

4	boneless, skinless chicken breasts	4
1	ripe pear, peeled, cored and cut into 1/4-inch (.5-cm) pieces	1
2 tsp.	Dijon mustard	10 ml
1	shallot, finely chopped	1
1/4 tsp.	salt	1.2 ml
1/4 cup	pear brandy	60 ml
1 Tbsp.	honey	15 ml
2 Tbsp.	chicken stock or water	30 ml
2 tsp.	finely chopped parsley	10 ml

Preheat the oven to 350°F (180°C). Place the chicken breasts in a single layer in a lightly buttered baking dish. Combine the remaining ingredients, except for the parsley, in a small bowl and pour evenly over the chicken. Cover with a lid or tin foil and bake for 15 minutes. Remove the cover and bake for 5 minutes more. Just before serving, sprinkle with the chopped parsley.

Grilled Chicken Breasts with Summer Bread Salad

I have been flogging this bread salad for years. It is an instant hit with everyone who tastes it. But don't go on my word alone. Try it for yourself and see.

Serves 6

6-8	boneless chicken breast halves, skin on	6-8
1/2 tsp.	salt	2.5 ml
2	cloves garlic, minced	2
2 Tbsp.	lemon juice	30 ml
1/2 tsp.	black pepper	2.5 ml
2 tsp.	fresh thyme leaves	10 ml
2 Tbsp.	olive oil	30 ml

Combine all the ingredients except the chicken and mix well. Add the chicken breasts and stir to coat with the marinade. Refrigerate for 4-12 hours.

Preheat the barbecue to medium. Grill skin side down until crisp. Turn over and grill until done, about 5 minutes. Arrange the bread salad on a platter and place the chicken on the salad. Serve immediately.

Summer Bread Salad

2 Tbsp.	lemon juice	30 ml
3/4 tsp.	salt	4 ml
1	clove garlic, minced	1
1/2 cup	olive oil	125 ml
1/2 tsp.	ground black pepper	2.5 ml
1 tsp.	ground cinnamon	5 ml
1/4 tsp.	ground allspice	1.2 ml
2 cups	crustless day-old bread, cubed	500 ml
1 cup	English cucumbers, cubed	250 ml
2/3 cup	red, green or yellow pepper, cubed	160 ml
1/2 cup	thinly sliced green, red or white onion	125 ml
4 cups	chopped parsley, loosely packed	1 L
2	medium tomatoes, diced	2

Whisk together the lemon juice, salt and garlic. Slowly beat in the olive oil, pepper, cinnamon and allspice. (The dressing may be prepared up to 12 hours ahead. Cover and refrigerate.)

Preheat the oven to 350°F (180°C). Bake the bread cubes until golden brown, turning them every few minutes.

Assemble the cucumber, pepper, onion and parsley in a large bowl. Just before serving, add the tomatoes and dressing to the salad. Toss well. Add the bread and toss again.

Garlicky Chicken Fricassee with Peppers and Rosemary

Serve this chicken with the creamy polenta from the Braised Lamb Shanks, page 116, or steamed new red potatoes.

Serves 4

3 Tbsp.	olive oil	45 ml
1 Tbsp.	unsalted butter	15 ml
1	2 1/2-3 lb. (1-1.3 kg) chicken, cut into 8 pieces	1
	salt and pepper to taste	
8	cloves garlic, thinly sliced	8
1/3 cup	dry white wine	80 ml
2	large sprigs fresh rosemary	2
1 Tbsp.	apple cider vinegar	15 ml
1 1/2 cups	chicken stock or water	375 ml
1	large red pepper, cored and cut into 1-inch (2.5-cm) strips	1
1	large yellow pepper, cored and cut into 1-inch (2.5-cm) strips	1
2 Tbsp.	finely chopped parsley	30 ml

In a large, heavy frying pan, heat 2 Tbsp. (30 ml) of the olive oil and the unsalted butter over medium-high heat. Add the chicken pieces (you may have to do this in two batches) and brown well on all sides. Transfer the chicken to a platter and season with salt and pepper.

Remove all but 2 Tbsp. (30 ml) fat from the pan and add the sliced garlic. Sauté for a minute, then add the white wine and rosemary. Reduce by three-quarters, add the vinegar and boil for 1 minute. Return the chicken pieces to the pan and add the chicken stock or water. Lower the heat and cover tightly. Simmer the chicken for 25 minutes, turning once.

Preheat the oven to 350°F (180°C). Place the peppers on a large piece of aluminum foil, toss with the remaining tablespoon (15 ml) of the olive oil and season with salt and pepper. Close the foil over the peppers and bake for 5-10 minutes until tender. Remove from the oven and open the foil to cool the peppers.

When the chicken is done, transfer to a serving platter. Remove the fat from the cooking liquid and reduce over high heat until it thickens slightly. Season to taste. Add the peppers and parsley and pour over the chicken.

Grilled Turkey Breast with Tomato Cumin Vinaigrette

This is very good served with the Spicy Bean and Corn Salad, page 36.

Serves 4

2	large, ripe tomatoes, chopped	2
1	clove garlic, minced	1
1 tsp.	paprika	5 ml
3/4 cup	olive oil	185 ml
3 Tbsp.	red wine vinegar	45 ml
1 tsp.	salt	5 ml
1/2 tsp.	pepper	2.5 ml
1 1/2 tsp.	ground cumin	7.5 ml
8	2- to 3-oz. (60- to 90-g) turkey cutlets	8
	salt and pepper to taste	
	olive oil	

To make the vinaigrette, combine the tomatoes, garlic, paprika, oil, vinegar, salt, pepper and cumin in the work bowl of a blender or food processor. Purée until smooth. If you're making it by hand, chop the tomatoes to a pulp, then combine with the remaining ingredients.

Preheat the barbecue or broiler. Salt and pepper the turkey cutlets and lightly brush with olive oil. Grill or broil until the turkey is cooked through, 3-5 minutes per side. Transfer to a platter and drizzle with the vinaigrette.

Duck Breast with Rhubarb and Red Wine Sauce

Since rhubarb is one of the first spring vegetables, for me this dish signifies spring emerging from winter. Marinating the duck with the dry spice rub overnight firms the meat and adds a savory edge.

Serves 4

6	boneless duck breast halves	6
1 tsp.	fresh thyme leaves	5 ml
1 Tbsp.	thinly sliced garlic	15 ml
1/2 tsp.	coarsely ground black pepper	2.5 ml
1 1/2 tsp.	salt	7.5 ml

With a sharp knife score a diamond pattern on the skin side of the duck breasts without cutting through to the meat. Combine the remaining ingredients and sprinkle on both sides of the duck breasts. Place in a shallow dish. Cover and refrigerate overnight.

To cook the duck, preheat the oven to 400°F (200°C). Heat a heavy (preferably cast-iron) pan over medium-low heat. When the pan is hot, scrape the marinade from the duck breasts and place the duck skin-side down in the pan.

As it cooks, a lot of fat will render out of the skin and the breasts will shrink. Pour off the fat as it accumulates. When the skin is brown and crispy, remove the duck from the pan and place skin-side up on a baking pan.

Place the duck breasts in the oven and cook for 4 minutes. To serve, cut the duck diagonally against the grain into thin slices. Place on 4 heated plates, spoon the warm sauce around the duck and serve immediately.

Rhubarb and Red Wine Sauce

1 cup	thinly sliced rhubarb	250 ml
3 Tbsp.	granulated sugar	45 ml
2 Tbsp.	water	30 ml
1/2 cup	red wine, preferably the wine you are having with dinner	125 ml
1 cup	Veal Demi-Glace, page 200	250 ml
	salt and sugar to taste	

Combine the rhubarb, sugar and water in a small saucepan. Bring the mixture to a boil, then turn the heat to low and simmer until the rhubarb is tender. Remove from the heat.

In a small saucepan, reduce the red wine by half. Add the demi-glace and bring to a boil. Add the rhubarb mixture and remove from the heat. Taste and season with the salt and sugar. The sauce should have a pleasant sweet and sour tang. (The sauce may be cooled and refrigerated, covered, for up to 4 days. Just before serving, gently reheat the sauce over low heat.)

Herbed Cornish Hens Grilled Under a Brick

A simple summer dish. Placing a brick on each bird ensures even and speedy cooking.

Serves 4

4	Cornish hens	4
2	cloves garlic, minced	2
1 tsp.	salt	5 ml
1 tsp.	pepper	5 ml
2 tsp.	fresh thyme leaves	10 ml
2 tsp.	fresh rosemary leaves	10 ml
1 tsp.	fresh lavender leaves	5 ml
4 Tbsp.	lemon juice	60 ml
4 Tbsp.	olive oil	60 ml

Split each Cornish hen down the breast bone. Open up the hens, turn them skin-side up and flatten with the palm of your hand. Mix the remaining ingredients together and rub over the hens. Marinate for at least 2 hours or overnight.

Preheat the barbecue to medium low. Place the hens on the barbecue skin-side up and place a clean brick on top of each hen. Cook for 10-15 minutes until well browned. Turn the hens over and replace the brick. Cook for 10-15 minutes longer until the skin is crispy and the thigh juices run clear when pricked with a knife.

Meat

Barbecued Beef Skewers with Minted Yogurt

Also try these skewers with Potato, Garlic and Parsley Sauce, page 115, and Summer Bread Salad, page 93.

Serves 4

1 1/2 lbs.	beef sirloin	675 g
1 tsp.	salt	5 ml
1 tsp.	pepper	5 ml
2 Tbsp.	lemon juice	30 ml
2 tsp.	dried oregano	10 ml
2	cloves garlic, minced	2
2 cups	yogurt	500 ml
1/2 tsp.	salt	2.5 ml
1	clove garlic, minced	1
1/2 cup	mint leaves, coarsely chopped	125 ml

Trim the beef of fat and sinews. Cut into 1-inch (2.5-cm) cubes and place in a bowl. Add the salt, pepper, lemon juice, oregano and garlic and mix well. Marinate for at least 2 hours or overnight. Thread the beef onto 12 skewers.

Place the yogurt in a sieve lined with a coffee filter or double layer of cheesecloth. Place over a bowl to catch the drips and let sit for an hour. Remove the yogurt from the sieve and combine with the salt, garlic and mint.

Preheat the barbecue or broiler on high. Cook the beef skewers until brown and done to your liking, 3-5 minutes per side. Remove from the heat and serve with the minted yogurt.

Stir-Fried Beef with Tomatoes, Basil and Chilies

A quick and sophisticated kind of Sloppy Joe with Asian overtones. Serve with rice or bread. It's great eaten cold out of the fridge, spread on bread.

Serves 4

2 Tbsp.	vegetable oil	30 ml
6	cloves garlic, minced	6
2	fresh chilies, finely chopped	2
1 lb.	lean ground beef	450 g
1	large ripe tomato, diced	1
2 Tbsp.	soya sauce	30 ml
1 tsp.	sugar	5 ml
1 cup	fresh basil leaves, loosely packed	250 ml

In a large frying pan or wok, heat the oil over high heat. Stir-fry the garlic and chilies until golden. Mix in the beef, breaking it up with the back of a spoon, and stir-fry until the beef is cooked through. Add the tomato and cook until it softens. Add the soya sauce, sugar and basil and cook until the basil wilts.

Red Wine and Thyme Marinated Flank Steak

Cooked to medium rare and thinly sliced across the grain, flank is one of the tastiest steaks around. Serve with Horseradish Mashed Potatoes, page 126, and Red Swiss Chard with Bacon, Garlic and White Wine, page 132.

Serves 4

1/2 cup	red wine	125 ml
1 tsp.	salt	5 ml
4	shallots, finely chopped	4
1 tsp.	black pepper	5 ml
1 Tbsp.	fresh thyme leaves	15 ml
1 1/2 lbs.	flank steak	675 g

Combine wine and seasonings in a shallow dish that will accommodate the steak. Coat the steak with the marinade. Cover and refrigerate overnight.

Preheat the barbecue or broiler. Cook the steak until done to your liking, or 3-5 minutes per side. Remove from the heat and let it rest for a few minutes. Carve thinly across the grain and serve.

Beef Stew with Caramelized Winter Vegetables

I like to add vegetables separately to a stew because I find that cooking them with the stew makes the braising liquid too sweet. This method allows for contrast between the sweet vegetables and the savory juices. If you prefer, you may cook the vegetables until tender in water instead of caramelizing them.

Serves 8

1/4 cup	vegetable oil	60 ml
4 lbs.	stewing beef, cut into 2-inch (5-cm) cubes	2 kg
1 cup	diced onion	250 ml
1/2 cup	diced celery	125 ml
1/2 cup	diced carrot	125 ml
4	cloves garlic, minced	4
3 Tbsp.	flour	45 ml
4 cups	red wine	1 L
2 cups	stock or water	500 ml
4	sprigs fresh thyme	4
	salt and pepper to taste	
4	medium carrots, peeled, cut in half lengthwise and cut into 2-inch (5-cm) pieces	4
2	medium parsnips, peeled, cut in half lengthwise and cut into 2-inch (5-cm) pieces	2
2	small turnips, peeled and cut into 8 wedges each	2
2 Tbsp.	vegetable oil	30 ml
2	large onions, peeled and cut into 8 wedges each	2
1 Tbsp.	light brown sugar	15 ml
2 tsp.	Dijon mustard	10 ml

Heat the oil in a large frying pan over medium-high heat and fry the beef in batches, without overcrowding the pan, until browned on all sides. Remove the beef to a plate.

Sauté the onion, celery, carrot and garlic until they are lightly browned. Whisk in the flour and stir for a minute. Slowly whisk in the red wine and stock or water. Bring to a boil and add the beef, with any juice that has collected on the plate, and thyme. Boil for a few minutes, skimming off any foam that rises to the surface. Season very lightly with salt and pepper.

Turn down to a bare simmer, cover and cook until the beef is tender, 2-3 hours, adding water as necessary to keep the beef covered with liquid. When the meat is tender, check the consistency of the liquid and reduce over high heat if it seems too thin. Correct the seasoning.

Bring a large pot of water to a boil. Salt liberally and add the carrots, parsnips and turnips. Cook for 2 minutes and drain well. Heat the vegetable oil in a large frying pan over medium heat and sauté the cooked vegetables and the onions for a few minutes until the vegetables start to brown.

Add the brown sugar, turn the heat to low, and cover with a lid. Cook for 5-10 minutes, until the vegetables are just tender. Remove the lid and add the Dijon mustard. Turn the heat to medium and continue cooking until the juices evaporate and the vegetables are browned.

Reheat the meat and pour out on to a large platter. Surround the stew with the vegetables and serve. Horseradish Mashed Potatoes, page 126, and cozy blankets or a fire would be the perfect accompaniment.

Winter Beef Salad with Creamy Horseradish Dressing

I call this a winter salad because it uses vegetables that are still tasty in the winter.

Serves 6

1 3/4-2 lbs.	top sirloin or flank steak	800-900 g
2	medium cloves garlic, peeled	2
1/2 tsp.	salt	2.5 ml
1/2 tsp.	freshly ground black pepper	2.5 ml
1 Tbsp.	Worcestershire sauce	15 ml
2 Tbsp.	vegetable oil	30 ml
1/2 lb.	red-skinned potatoes	225 g
1/2 lb.	small beets	225 g
2	large bunches spinach, stemmed, washed and dried	2
1	medium red onion, sliced into thin rings	1

To prepare the meat, trim off the fat. If you are using flank steak, score it lightly on both sides in a diamond pattern at 2-inch (5-cm) intervals. Finely chop the garlic, then crush to a paste with the salt, using the flat of a knife. Combine the garlic with the pepper, Worcestershire sauce and oil. Rub the mixture on both sides of the steak. (The steak may be prepared to this point up to 2 days in advance. Cover and refrigerate until ready to cook.)

Cut the potatoes into 1/2-inch (1-cm) pieces and cook in salted water until tender. Drain and set aside. Cook the beets until tender and drain. When cool enough to handle, cut them into 1/2-inch (1-cm) wedges.

Place the spinach on a large platter or two. Arrange the beets, potatoes and red onions over the spinach.

Heat a heavy, preferably cast-iron pan over medium heat. When it is hot, slip in the steak. Cook until browned on one side, approximately 4-5 minutes. If the steak is browning too quickly, adjust the heat accordingly. Turn the steak over and brown the other side. Continue cooking the steak until it is done to your liking. Remove from the pan and let rest for 5 minutes.

Slice the steak thinly across the grain and arrange on the salad. Serve immediately with the dressing on the side.

Creamy Horseradish Dressing

1/2 cup	cider vinegar	125 ml
2 Tbsp.	Dijon mustard	30 ml
1/2 tsp.	salt	2.5 ml
1 Tbsp.	honey	15 ml
6 Tbsp.	fresh horseradish, grated, or 4 Tbsp. (60 ml) prepared horseradish	90 ml
2 cups	sour cream or Crème Fraîche, page 192	500 ml
1/2 cup	water	125 ml

To make the dressing, combine all the ingredients in a bowl and whisk until smooth. (It can be prepared 3 days in advance. Cover and refrigerate.)

Venison with Sun-Dried Sour Cherry and Blue Cheese Butter

I wasn't a big fan of venison until I tried it with this sauce. With a pile of garlicky mashed potatoes . . . heaven. You can substitute lamb for the venison if you wish.

Serves 4

1/4 cup	red wine	60 ml
1/4 cup	sun-dried sour cherries	60 ml
1/4 lb.	unsalted butter, softened	115 g
2 Tbsp.	honey	30 ml
1/4 cup	blue cheese, crumbled	60 ml
1 Tbsp.	vegetable oil	15 ml
8	3-oz. (90-g) venison medallions	8

To make the butter, place the red wine and cherries in a small pot and bring to a boil. Cover and remove from the heat. Cool. With a mixer or whisk whip the butter until light. Mix in the honey, blue cheese and cooled cherry mixture. Place in a container, cover and refrigerate overnight. (The butter can be made up to a week in advance.) Bring to room temperature before using.

Heat the oil in a skillet large enough to hold the venison in a single layer. Over high heat, sear the meat on both sides until medium rare, about 1 1/2 minutes total cooking time.

Place the venison on heated plates or a large platter and top with the butter. Serve immediately.

Rabbit Sausages

I always feel satisfied and comforted after completing a round of sausage-making. There is something very fundamental about it and you have the satisfaction of knowing what your sausages are made from. I usually double the recipe so I'll have some to give away to sausage-loving friends. Serve with Dried Fruit Mustard, page 197, or Sour and Sweet Cherry Ketchup, page 195.

Makes about 6 lbs. (2.7 kg)

1 3/4 lbs.	rabbit meat (trimmings are good to use here)	800 g
1 3/4 lbs.	lean pork butt	800 g
1 3/4 lbs.	pork fat	800 g
	the rabbit liver and kidneys	
1 Tbsp.	salt	15 ml
1 tsp.	fennel seeds	5 ml
1 tsp.	coarsely crushed black pepper	5 ml
4	medium cloves garlic, minced	4
20	fresh sage leaves	20
3 yards	natural casings	3 meters

Cut the meat into 1-inch (2.5-cm) cubes and combine with all the other stuffing ingredients. Mix well. Cover and refrigerate overnight.

The next day, grind half of the meat mixture finely and the other half coarsely. Blend together well and stuff into the casings. The sausages keep 2-3 days refrigerated. Freeze for longer storage.

(If you don't want to make rabbit sausages, use pork butt instead of the rabbit meat. Duck sausages can be made by substituting duck meat and using 1 Tbsp. (15 ml) fresh thyme leaves instead of the sage; lamb by using it in place of the rabbit and adding 1 Tbsp. (15 ml) fresh rosemary leaves instead of the sage.)

Braised Rabbit Sausages with Dried Pears and Sauerkraut

This is a version of a dish that my friend Michael made for Christmas dinner one year. He spent days traveling around town finding different kinds of sausages and cured meats to go in it. It was well worth the effort and made for an abundant and joyous celebration. Salt-pickled sauerkraut is available in eastern European delicatessens.

Serves 6-8

2 1/2 lbs.	salt-pickled sauerkraut	1 kg
12	Rabbit Sausages, opposite, or your favorite pork sausage (not breakfast sausages)	12
1 Tbsp.	vegetable oil	15 ml
2	medium onions, diced	2
1 1/2 cups	Riesling wine	375 ml
1/2 lb.	dried pears, cut into 1/2-inch (1-cm) strips	225 g
2 tsp.	caraway seeds	10 ml
2 Tbsp.	honey	30 ml
	salt and pepper to taste	

Soak the sauerkraut in cold water for 1/2 hour. Squeeze dry and place in a large ovenproof pot or casserole dish with a lid.

Over medium heat, brown the sausages in the vegetable oil on all sides. Remove from the pan and set aside.

Pour off all but 4 Tbsp. (60 ml) of the fat. Add the onions and sauté until translucent. Add the wine and bring to a boil, scraping up any brown bits clinging to the bottom of the pan. Pour over the sauerkraut. Add the pears, caraway seeds and honey to the sauerkraut and mix well. Cover with the lid and place in a 325°F (160°C) oven for 1 1/2 hours, stirring every half-hour. The sauerkraut should be tender by then and the wine almost evaporated. If not, bake for 1/2 hour longer, adding more wine if needed.

Taste for seasoning and add salt and pepper if necessary. Tuck the sausages into the sauerkraut. Cover and bake for 1/2 hour more.

To serve, remove the sausages and mound the cabbage onto a large platter. Cut the sausages in half on the diagonal and arrange on the cabbage. Serve with small boiled red-skinned potatoes that have been tossed with a little butter, a good crusty loaf of bread and bowls of Dijon and grainy mustard.

Seared Rabbit with Mustard and Fennel

This rabbit goes perfectly with the Blue Cheese and Spinach Tart, page 131, or the Mashed Sweet Potatoes with Blue Cheese, page 124. Save the liver, kidneys and heart, and trim the meat from the front legs to make Rabbit Sausages, page 106.

Serves 6

3	rabbits, 2 to 2 1/2 lbs. (about 1 kg)	3
3 Tbsp.	Dijon mustard	45 ml
3/4 tsp.	salt	4 ml
1 1/2 tsp.	coarsely crushed fennel seeds	7.5 ml
2 Tbsp.	finely minced shallots	30 ml
1/2 tsp.	ground black pepper	2.5 ml
2 Tbsp.	vegetable oil	30 ml
1/2 cup	white wine	125 ml

Remove the leg and thigh portions from the rabbits in one piece and debone the thigh. Set aside. Debone the loin. You may want to get an accommodating butcher to do this for you; if you're doing it yourself, imagine the rabbit is an elongated chicken and the loin is the breast.

Place the legs and loins in a bowl and add the mustard, salt, fennel, shallots and pepper. Mix well, cover and refrigerate overnight.

Preheat the oven to 350°F (180°C). Heat the vegetable oil in a large, heavy frying pan over medium-high heat. Add the legs and sear on both sides until brown. Remove the legs to a baking sheet. Add the loins to the frying pan and sear until brown on all sides. Remove to a plate. Deglaze the pan with the white wine, scraping up the browned bits, and pour over the rabbit legs. (The rabbit may be prepared up to this point 2 hours in advance.) Bake the legs for 15 minutes, then add the loins and bake for 5 minutes more. Serve on heated plates with the pan juices.

Andrew's Brined Pork Loin with Tomato and Ginger Jam

Fellow chef Andrew has a great love of far eastern spicing and flavors. This particular combination of ingredients is his. Lightly sautéed spinach would go well with this dish.

Serves 6-8

2 1/2 lbs.	boneless pork loin	1 kg
1 recipe	Sweetly Spiced Brine for Pork	1 recipe
1 Tbsp.	vegetable oil	15 ml
	Tomato and Ginger Jam, page 194	

With a skewer, prick the pork loin crosswise all the way through about 20 times. Place the pork in a narrow container and pour the brine over it. Cover and refrigerate for 3-5 days, keeping in mind that the flavor will get stronger the longer the pork sits in the brine.

When you are ready to cook the pork, preheat the oven to 350°F (180°C). Remove the pork from the brine and pat dry. Heat the vegetable oil in a large frying pan over medium-high heat. Add the pork loin and brown on all sides. Transfer to a baking pan and bake for 30 minutes. Let the pork rest for 10 minutes before slicing and serving with Tomato and Ginger Jam.

Sweetly Spiced Brine for Pork

4 cups	water	1 L
1/4 cup	salt	60 ml
1/2 cup	sugar	125 ml
	zest of 1 orange	
1	8-inch (20-cm) cinnamon stick, crumbled	1
2 tsp.	whole black peppercorns	10 ml
2 tsp.	whole white peppercorns	10 ml
16	whole star anise, crushed	16
10	1/4-inch (.5-cm) slices ginger, lightly crushed	10

Combine all the ingredients in a saucepan and bring to a boil. Remove from the heat and cool completely before using. Use immediately.

Pork Tenderloin with Sautéed Red Cabbage and Apples

Pork and cabbage are a time-tested duo. Pork, cabbage and apples are a very compatible threesome indeed. A great winter dish.

Serves 4

2	pork tenderloins, about 1 1/2 lbs. (675 g) total	2
1 Tbsp.	vegetable oil	15 ml
	salt and pepper to taste	
2 Tbsp.	shallots, finely chopped	30 ml
2 cups	red cabbage, thinly sliced	500 ml
1/2 cup	apple, peeled, cored and thinly sliced	125 ml
2 tsp.	Dijon mustard	10 ml
2 tsp.	grainy mustard	10 ml
1 Tbsp.	honey	15 ml
1 Tbsp.	cider vinegar	15 ml
	salt and pepper to taste	

Preheat the oven to 350°F (180°C). In a frying pan over medium-high heat, sauté the pork tenderloin in oil until browned on all sides. Place on a baking sheet and season with salt and pepper.

In the same pan, sauté the shallots over medium heat until translucent. Add the cabbage and apple and sauté until slightly wilted. Mix in the Dijon mustard, grainy mustard, honey and cider vinegar. Season with salt and pepper and set aside.

Bake the tenderloin for 15 minutes. Remove from the oven and let rest for 5 minutes. Reheat the cabbage mixture. Slice the pork tenderloin. Place the cabbage and tenderloin on a heated platter or plates and serve immediately.

Pepper and Garlic Cured Pork Chops

My love of charcuterie inspired me to experiment with dry-curing meats. These pork chops take on a hint of sausage flavor that is quite appealing. Try them with Sour and Sweet Cherry or Blackberry Ketchup, page 195 (and mashed potatoes, of course).

Serves 6

1 1/2 tsp.	black peppercorns	7.5 ml
1 Tbsp.	coriander seeds	15 ml
1 Tbsp.	salt	15 ml
1 1/2 tsp.	sugar	7.5 ml
6	cloves garlic, peeled and thinly sliced	6
6	1-inch-thick (2.5-cm) rack pork chops or center-cut pork chops	6
1 Tbsp.	vegetable oil	15 ml

Coarsely crush the black peppercorns and coriander seeds and combine with the salt and sugar.

In a dish large enough to hold the pork chops in a single layer, sprinkle half the salt mixture and half the garlic. Place the chops in the dish and sprinkle with the remaining salt mixture and garlic, pressing it in with your fingers. Cover tightly and refrigerate for 2-3 days.

When you are ready to cook the chops, scrape the marinade from them. Preheat the oven to 350°F (180°C). Heat the vegetable oil in a heavy skillet over medium-high heat. Brown the chops well on both sides and place them in a single layer in a baking pan. Bake for 8-10 minutes. Serve immediately.

Lamb Braised with Yogurt, Dill and Cilantro

I love this dish. The cilantro and dill blend together to create an intriguing new flavor that fragrantly complements the lamb.

Serves 6

3 lbs.	boneless lamb shoulder	1.3 kg
4	1-inch (2.5-cm) cubes of fresh ginger, coarsely chopped	4
8	medium cloves garlic, peeled and crushed	8
1/2 cup	water	125 ml
4 Tbsp.	vegetable oil	60 ml
3	large onions, thinly sliced into half moons	3
2 cups	plain yogurt	500 ml
1 tsp.	salt	5 ml
1 cup	coarsely chopped fresh cilantro leaves, well packed	250 ml
1 cup	chopped dill, well packed	250 ml
1/2 cup	water	125 ml
1 tsp.	ground black pepper	5 ml

Cut the lamb into 1 1/2-inch (4-cm) pieces.

Blend the ginger, garlic and water in a food processor or blender.

Heat the oil in a heavy, wide pot over medium-high heat. Fry the onions until they brown lightly in a few spots. Add the lamb and fry until it too picks up a few brown spots. Stir in the ginger-garlic paste and cook and stir for about 10 minutes, until it has browned lightly. Mix in the yogurt and scrape up any browned bits clinging to the pan. Add the salt and enough water to cover the lamb by 1 inch (2.5 cm). Lower the heat to a bare simmer, cover and cook for 1 1/2-2 hours, replenishing the water as necessary, until the lamb is tender. (The lamb may be prepared to this point up to 2 days in advance. Cool, cover and refrigerate. Remove any fat that rises to the top before continuing with the next step.)

When the lamb is tender, cook uncovered on high heat until the sauce is reduced to a heavy cream consistency.

You Say Coriander, I Say Cilantro

Coriander and cilantro are one and the same. Coriander is the name used in the east and cilantro in the west. When I first moved here I had to train myself to say cilantro. When I said coriander people thought that I meant the seeds.

Place the cilantro and dill in a food processor or blender with the 1/2 cup (125 ml) water and blend until smooth.

Spoon off any fat that has collected on the top of the lamb. Stir in the cilantro and dill purée and black pepper. Adjust the seasoning if necessary. Serve with rice, potatoes or a crusty bread to mop up the delicious sauce.

Grilled Leg of Lamb with Herb and Spice Crust

Serve it with Red Lettuce with Roasted Peppers, Feta and Marjoram Vinaigrette, page 30.

Serves 6-8

1/4 cup	olive oil	60 ml
6	cloves garlic, finely chopped	6
1 Tbsp.	coriander seed	15 ml
1 Tbsp.	black peppercorns	15 ml
2 tsp.	fennel seeds	10 ml
1 Tbsp.	fresh thyme leaves	15 ml
1 Tbsp.	fresh rosemary leaves	15 ml
1 1/2 tsp.	salt	7.5 ml
1	butterflied leg of lamb, 3 1/2-4 lbs. (1.5-2 kg)	1

Combine the olive oil and garlic. Coarsely grind the coriander, pepper and fennel in a spice or coffee grinder, or use a mortar and pestle. Add to the oil along with the thyme, rosemary and salt. Spread the mixture over the lamb. Cover and refrigerate overnight.

Preheat the oven or barbecue to 350°F (180°C). Bake or grill the lamb for approximately 30-45 minutes, until medium rare. Cover loosely with foil and let rest for 10-15 minutes before carving.

Carve the lamb into thin slices across the grain and arrange on a warm platter. Serve immediately.

Grilled Lamb Salad with Rhubarb Vinaigrette

Spring lamb, spring rhubarb. Although formulated on a whim, the flavors are truly harmonious.

Serves 6

3 Tbsp.	Rhubarb Compote, page 167	45 ml
3 Tbsp.	Dijon mustard	45 ml
1/2 tsp.	salt	2.5 ml
2 tsp.	sugar	10 ml
1 Tbsp.	apple cider vinegar	15 ml
1/2 cup	vegetable oil	125 ml
8	cloves garlic, finely chopped	8
2 Tbsp.	coarsely crushed black peppercorns	30 ml
2 tsp.	coarsely crushed fennel seeds	10 ml
1 tsp.	salt	5 ml
4 Tbsp.	vegetable oil	60 ml
1 1/2 lbs.	boneless, butterflied lamb leg	675 g
1 1/2 lbs.	washed and dried, strongly flavored salad greens, such as arugula, radicchio, Belgian endive, curly chicory, escarole	675 g

To make the dressing, whisk together the rhubarb compote, mustard, salt, sugar and vinegar. Slowly beat in the oil to emulsify. Cover and refrigerate until ready to use. Combine the garlic, peppercorns, fennel, salt and vegetable oil. Spread over the lamb and marinate for at least 2 hours or overnight in the refrigerator.

Preheat the barbecue or broiler. Grill or broil the lamb for 10-15 minutes on each side for medium rare. Remove from the heat and let the lamb rest for 10 minutes.

Toss the salad greens with the dressing and place on individual plates or a large serving platter. Thinly slice the lamb and arrange on the salad. Serve immediately.

Grilled Lamb Leg with Potato, Garlic and Parsley Sauce

This cold potato sauce is a perfect summer accompaniment to grilled lamb. To round out the meal, all you need is a platter of sliced ripe tomatoes, cucumbers, onions and fennel and a loaf of good bread to slice thickly and grill on the barbecue after the lamb is done.

Serves 6

1 Tbsp.	fresh thyme leaves	15 ml
1 tsp.	salt	5 ml
1 tsp.	cracked black pepper	5 ml
2 Tbsp.	olive oil	30 ml
1	butterflied lamb leg, 2 1/2-3 lbs. (1-1.3 kg)	1

Combine the thyme, salt, pepper and olive oil and spread over the lamb leg. (The lamb may be prepared up to 48 hours in advance. Cover and refrigerate.) Grill on a preheated, medium-low barbecue, about 15-20 minutes per side for medium rare. Remove from the grill and let rest for 10 minutes. Slice and arrange on a platter. Serve the potato sauce on the side.

Potato, Garlic and Parsley Sauce

1 lb.	small unpeeled new potatoes	450 g
4	medium cloves garlic, peeled	4
1 tsp.	salt	5 ml
1/2 cup	olive oil	125 ml
1/4 cup	lemon juice	60 ml
1 Tbsp.	finely chopped parsley	15 ml
	black pepper to taste	

Cover the potatoes with water and bring to a boil. Cook until the potatoes are tender, 20-30 minutes.

While the potatoes are cooking, finely chop the garlic and mash it with the salt until pasty, using the flat of the knife. When the potatoes are cool enough to handle, peel and press through a ricer or mash by hand until smooth. (If you use a food processor, the potatoes will become a gluey mess.) Slowly beat in the olive oil. Stir in the lemon juice, mashed garlic and parsley and season with black pepper. Cover and refrigerate until ready to use. (The sauce may be made 1 day in advance.)

Braised Lamb Shanks with Creamy Polenta

Lamb shanks have become more popular in recent years. This is my favorite way to prepare them. If you don't have the patience for making polenta, serve them with a small pasta shape such as orzo, mashed potatoes or a good bread.

Serves 4-6

6	lamb shanks	6
2 cups	red wine	500 ml
1	28-oz. (796-ml) can whole plum tomatoes, drained, puréed and sieved to remove the seeds	1
8 cups	chicken stock or water	2 L
3 Tbsp.	vegetable oil	45 ml
4	medium cloves garlic, minced	4
1 1/2 cups	onion, finely diced	375 ml
3/4 cup	celery, finely diced	185 ml
3/4 cup	carrots, finely diced	185 ml
1 Tbsp.	parsley, finely chopped	15 ml
1	bay leaf	1
1 tsp.	salt	5 ml
3 Tbsp.	parsley, finely chopped	45 ml
1 tsp.	garlic, minced	5 ml
	the finely grated peel of one lemon	
10 cups	water	2.5 L
2 tsp.	salt	10 ml
2 cups	cornmeal	500 ml
6 Tbsp.	butter	90 ml
2 cups	grated Parmesan cheese	500 ml

Preheat the oven to 300°F (150°C). Trim any visible fat from the lamb shanks. Rinse, pat dry and place them in an ovenproof pot large enough to hold them in a single layer. Add the red wine, tomatoes and the stock or water (use enough to cover the shanks by 2 inches/5 cm). Bring to a boil.

While waiting for the lamb shanks to boil, heat the vegetable oil in a frying pan over medium heat. Sauté the garlic, onion, celery, carrots and 1 Tbsp. (15 ml) parsley until the vegetables are lightly browned. Set aside.

When the lamb shanks come to a boil, turn the heat down to a simmer and skim off any foam that rises to the top. Add the sautéed vegetables, bay leaf and salt. Cover and place in the oven.

Bake for 2 1/2 hours, checking occasionally to make sure the liquid is covering the lamb shanks. If not, use water to top up the liquid.

Combine the 3 Tbsp. (45 ml) parsley, garlic and lemon peel. Cover and refrigerate.

When the lamb shanks have cooked for 1 1/2 hours, start the polenta. Bring the water and salt to a boil in a large, wide, heavy-bottomed pot. Stirring constantly, add the cornmeal in a slow steady stream. Turn the heat to medium low and cook at a lively simmer for 1 hour, stirring occasionally. Remove from the heat and cover.

Remove the lamb shanks from the oven. Take the meat out of the liquid and cover. Strain the liquid through a sieve and reserve. Force the vegetables through the sieve or purée them in a food processor until smooth. Add the puréed vegetables to the liquid and boil over high heat until it starts to thicken.

Return the shanks to the pot. (The shanks may be cooked to this point up to 2 days in advance. Cool, cover and refrigerate.) Simmer the shanks for 1/2 hour. If you are reheating the shanks after being refrigerated, slowly bring to a simmer then simmer for 1/2 hour.

While the shanks are simmering, finish the polenta. Slowly reheat the cornmeal mixture, stirring occasionally. Add the butter and Parmesan cheese and stir until the butter is melted. Serve the shanks with the polenta and pass the parsley, garlic and lemon garnish.

Grilled Lamb Shanks with Garlic and Oregano Glaze

If you like tender, succulent, falling-off-the-bone lamb, with a crusty outside, this is the ideal dish for you.

Serves 4-6

6	lamb shanks	6
4	medium cloves garlic, peeled and cut in half	4
1	small onion, cut in half	1
1/2 tsp.	salt	2.5 ml
30	medium cloves garlic, unpeeled	30
2 Tbsp.	oregano	30 ml
1 tsp.	salt	5 ml
	pepper to taste	

Trim the shanks of excess fat and place in a large pot. Add enough water to cover the shanks by 2 inches (5 cm) and bring to a boil. Skim off any foam that rises to the top and turn the heat down to a simmer. Add the 4 cloves of garlic, the onion and salt. Cook the shanks for 3 hours, until they are extremely tender, adding more water if necessary.

While the shanks cook, place the unpeeled garlic in a heavy frying pan over medium heat. Brown the cloves on all sides; this will caramelize the garlic inside the husks and give it a rich, nutty flavor. A few charred spots here and there are fine. Patience is important. Turn the cloves as they become browned on one side and remove each clove as it is done. Cool the cloves before peeling.

When the shanks have finished cooking, remove them from the pot and place them in a single layer in a shallow oven-proof dish. Reserve 1/2 cup (125 ml) of the broth. Blend the garlic, broth, oregano, salt and pepper to a paste in the work bowl of a food processor. Pour the paste over the lamb shanks and turn to coat each one with the marinade. Marinate for 1 hour. (The shanks may be prepared to this point up to 1 day in advance. Cover and refrigerate overnight. Bring to room temperature before continuing.)

Preheat the broiler or barbecue. If you broil the shanks, broil slowly, at least 12 inches (30 cm) from the heat. If you barbecue, grill on low heat. Turn the meat as it cooks, so it is crusty and brown all over. Serve immediately, but watch for the protruding bone, which is extremely hot!

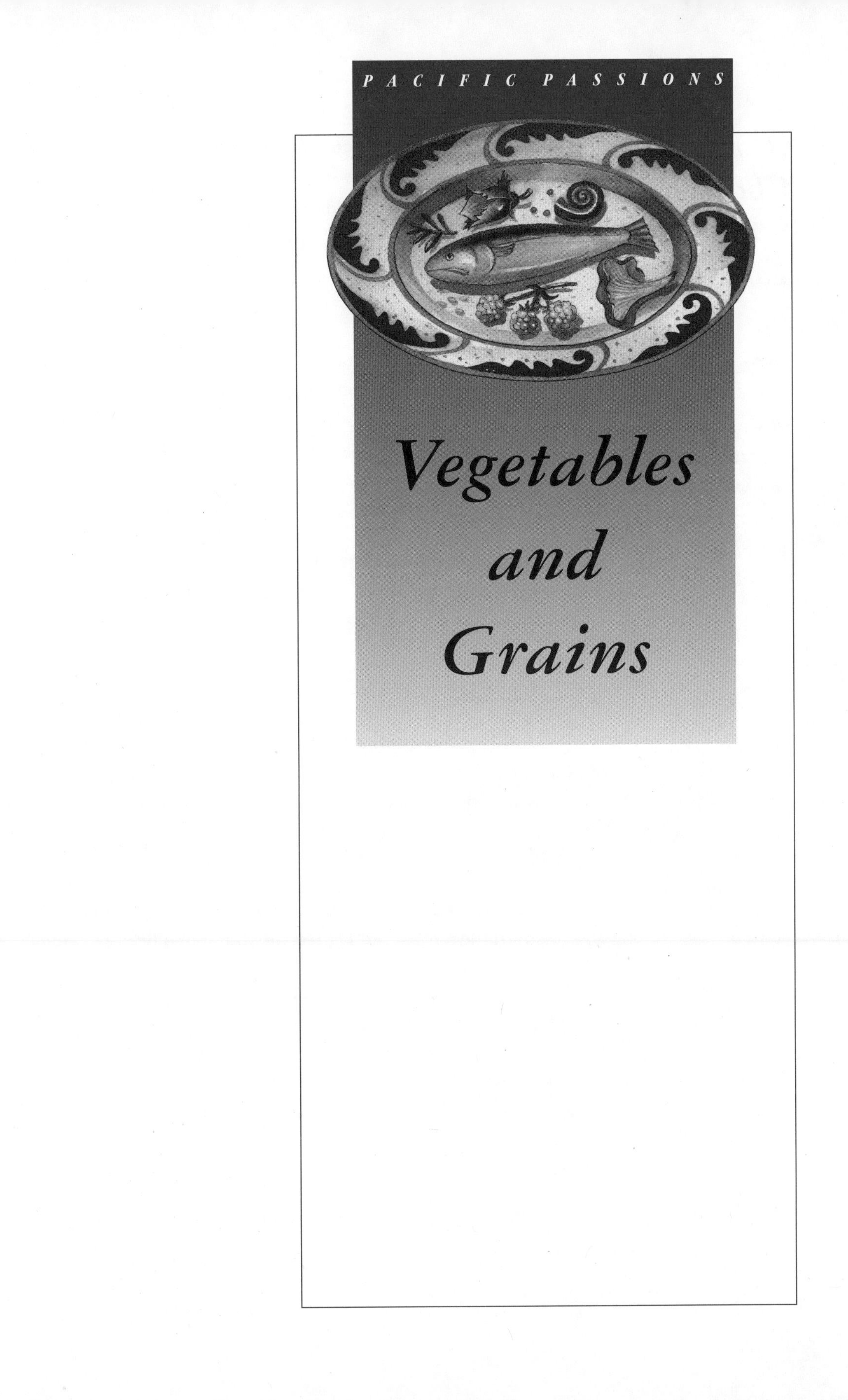

Vegetables and Grains

Quark, Charred Scallion and Tomato Tart

Quark is a dry, slightly grainy cream cheese with a pleasant tang that is available in most supermarkets. Try serving the tart with a big, juicy rack of lamb if you want to be really fancy.

Makes 1 9-inch (22-cm) tart, serving 6-8

2	bunches green onions	2
1	large onion, diced	1
1 Tbsp.	butter	15 ml
2	eggs	2
1 lb.	quark	450 g
3/4 tsp.	salt	4 ml
3/4 tsp.	coarsely ground black pepper	4 ml
2	medium tomatoes, sliced into 4 slices each	2
1 tsp.	fresh thyme leaves	5 ml
1	9-inch (22-cm) baked tart shell (see Savory Pastry, page 190)	1

Wash and dry the green onions and trim the stem end. Spread out in a single layer on a baking sheet and broil until the onions are lightly charred. Cool and chop coarsely.

Sauté the onions in the butter over medium-low heat until translucent.

In a food processor or by hand, blend the eggs into the quark, one at a time. Remove from the food processor and stir in the onions, salt and pepper and mix well.

Pour evenly into the prebaked tart shell. Arrange the tomatoes in a pleasing pattern on top of the filling. Sprinkle with the fresh thyme leaves. Bake for 30 minutes until the tart has set. Let rest for 10 minutes before serving.

Grilled Sui Choy with Mustard and Caraway

Make this in the summer when you can find small sui choy. Most of the flavor of this dish comes from grilling as much of the surface area as possible.

Serves 6

2 lbs.	sui choy	900 g
1/2 cup	Dijon mustard	125 ml
1/4 cup	water	60 ml
2 Tbsp.	vegetable oil	30 ml
1 tsp.	caraway seeds	5 ml
	pepper to taste	

Preheat the barbecue to medium high. Remove the outer leaves of the sui choy and cut them into quarters.

Mix the remaining ingredients in a large bowl. Add the sui choy and toss well to coat with the Dijon mixture. Place the cabbage on the grill and cook until deeply marked on all sides. Transfer to a platter and serve.

Scalloped Savoy Cabbage

This dish received raves at a harvest dinner conceived by my husband Steven, where it was served with rotisserie-cooked turkey and venison sausages.

Serves 6-8 generously

1	2-lb. (900-g) savoy cabbage	1
2 cups	thinly sliced onions	500 ml
4 cups	whipping cream	1 L
1 cup	18% cream	250 ml
1 1/2 tsp.	salt	7.5 ml
	pepper to taste	

Remove and discard the outer leaves of the cabbage and cut it into quarters. Core and thinly slice the cabbage. Place in a bowl and toss with the onions. Transfer to a deep 9- by 13-inch (22- by 33-cm) baking dish.

Preheat the oven to 350°F (180°C). Bring the creams, salt and pepper to a boil. Pour over the cabbage and cover tightly with tin foil or with a lid. Place on a baking pan that has also been covered with tin foil (to protect from drips). Place in the oven and bake for 45 minutes. Remove the lid and bake for 30 minutes longer. Remove from the oven and let the dish sit for 10 minutes before serving.

Spaghetti Squash with Roasted Garlic and Sun-Dried Tomatoes

This summery vegetable dish may be served either hot, or cold as a salad.

Serves 4-6

1	small spaghetti squash, about 2 lbs. (900 g)	1
1/2 cup	water	125 ml
1 1/2 Tbsp.	cider vinegar	20 ml
1/2 tsp.	salt	2.5 ml
1/4 tsp.	ground black pepper	1.2 ml
3	sun-dried tomatoes, rehydrated or oil-packed	3
10	cloves roasted garlic, page 196	10
1/2 cup	olive oil	125 ml
2	medium, ripe tomatoes, seeded and diced into 1/4-inch (.6-cm) pieces	2
1/2 cup	chopped parsley	125 ml
1/4 cup	basil leaves, torn into small pieces	60 ml

Preheat the oven to 350°F (180°C). Cut the squash in half and place cut side down in a baking dish. Pour the water around the squash and cover tightly with tin foil or a lid. Bake for about 1 hour until tender.

While the squash is baking, prepare the rest of the ingredients. To make the dressing, purée the vinegar, salt, pepper, sun-dried tomatoes and garlic in the work bowl of a food processor or blender. With the motor on, add the olive oil in a slow steady stream. Transfer to a bowl.

When the squash is done, scrape it from the shell into a bowl. Toss with the dressing. If you are serving the squash hot, combine with the remaining ingredients and serve immediately. If you are serving it cold, let it cool to room temperature then toss with the tomatoes, parsley and basil.

Butternut Squash and Onion Pie with a Millet Crust

Serves 6

3/4 cup	millet	185 ml
1 1/2 cups	water	375 ml
1/8 tsp.	salt	.5 ml
2 Tbsp.	unsalted butter	30 ml
1 1/2 cups	onion, thinly sliced	375 ml
1-2 lbs.	butternut squash	450-900 g
	salt and pepper to taste	
1	large egg	1
1/2 tsp.	cumin seed	2.5 ml
	a large pinch each of ground dried ginger, cinnamon and nutmeg	

Heat a heavy frying pan over medium heat and roast the millet, stirring or shaking the pan constantly until the millet is flecked with brown spots. Transfer to a pot with the water and salt. Bring to a boil, cover and cook over low heat for 40 minutes, until the millet is tender. Remove from the heat and fluff with a fork.

Melt the butter in a frying pan over medium heat and sauté the onion until brown. Set aside.

Peel the squash and cut into 1-inch (2.5-cm) pieces. Cover with water and cook over high heat until tender. Drain and purée in a food processor or blender. Scrape into a bowl and season with salt and pepper.

Beat the egg, the browned onion and the spices into the squash.

Preheat the oven to 350°F (180°C). Lightly oil a 9-inch (22-cm) deep pie pan and press the millet evenly into the pan to form a crust. Spread the squash mixture over the millet. Bake for 40 minutes until set. Serve hot or at room temperature.

Mashed Sweet Potatoes with Blue Cheese

I like to demonstrate this recipe in cooking classes as it wins instant converts. Remember this one the next time you serve turkey.

Serves 4-6

3	large sweet potatoes, or yams, about 2 lbs. (900 g), peeled and cut into 1-inch (2.5-cm) cubes	3
4 Tbsp.	unsalted butter	60 ml
	salt and pepper to taste	
1 cup	crumbled blue cheese	250 ml

Cook the sweet potatoes in boiling water until tender, about 25 minutes. Drain.

Mash by hand if you like a chunky texture or purée in a food processor. Add the butter. Season with salt and pepper and stir in the blue cheese. (The potatoes may be prepared a day in advance and reheated over low heat on top of the stove or in a microwave oven. Stir in the blue cheese just before serving.)

Decadent Scalloped Potatoes

Our friend Michael was enthusiastic about these potatoes but commented that they were not burnt enough—the way he enjoyed them growing up. Sometimes sentimentality surpasses cultivated adult taste buds and he went home with a pan of potatoes to burn at his leisure. If you share his sentiment, by all means cook them until burnt!

Serves 6-8 generously

3 lbs.	medium red-skinned potatoes, peeled	1.3 kg
1	medium clove garlic, minced	1
1 1/4 tsp.	salt	6.2 ml
1/2 tsp.	pepper	2.5 ml
1 cup	freshly grated Parmesan cheese	250 ml
3 cups	whipping cream	750 ml
1 cup	18% cream	250 ml

Preheat the oven to 350°F (180°C). Thinly slice the potatoes as if making potato chips. Mash the garlic to a paste with some of the salt. Add to the potatoes with the rest of the salt, pepper and Parmesan cheese. Toss the potatoes well and place in a deep 9- by 13-inch (22- by 33-cm) baking dish.

Combine the creams in a saucepan and bring to a boil. Pour over the potatoes and cover tightly with tin foil. Place the baking dish on a pan that you have also covered with foil (to protect from drips). Bake covered for 1 hour. Remove the foil from the top of the potatoes and bake for 1/2 hour longer until golden brown.

A "Mess" of Potatoes, Rapini and Chorizo Sausage

Rapini, also known as broccoli rabe, appears in winter and early spring. As with most winter greens, cooking until tender brings out the sweet mellow flavor. Serve it with Pan-Roasted Flounder with Garlic and Chilies, page 80. This dish can be cooked without the chorizo if you prefer. It is sublime tossed with a crumbling of goat cheese before it leaves the pot.

Serves 4-6

1	raw, unsmoked chorizo sausage	1
1 1/2 lbs.	rapini	375 g
1 Tbsp.	olive oil	15 ml
1 lb.	red-skinned potatoes, unpeeled, sliced 1/4 inch (.6 cm) thick	450 g
2 cups	water, lightly salted	500 ml
	salt and pepper to taste	
	lemon wedges	

Remove the sausage from its casing and set aside. Pluck the leaves, tender stems and florets from the rapini and discard the tough stalks. Wash and drain the leaves and florets.

Heat the olive oil in a saucepan over medium heat and sauté the chorizo until it loses its raw color. Add the potatoes and salted water. Bring to a boil and cook until tender, about 20-30 minutes. The liquid will reduce as the potatoes cook, but if they look like they are in danger of drying out, add another 1/2 cup (125 ml) of water.

When the potatoes are tender, add the rapini. There should be about 1/2 cup (125 ml) of liquid left in the pot. Add water if needed. Cover and cook for about 10 minutes over medium heat, stirring occasionally, until the rapini is tender. Season with salt and pepper, and serve with the lemon wedges.

Horseradish Mashed Potatoes

Yes, I know—these are Oprah's favorite. Thank goodness! Without her these potatoes would never have achieved the popularity they deserve.

Makes about 4 cups (1 L)

2 lbs.	russet or Yukon gold potatoes, peeled and cut into 1-inch (2.5-cm) cubes	900 g
2 tsp.	salt	10 ml
4 Tbsp.	unsalted butter	60 ml
1/2 cup	hot milk	125 ml
1 Tbsp.	prepared horseradish	15 ml
	salt and pepper to taste	

Place the potatoes in a large pot with enough cold water to cover them by 4 inches (10 cm). Bring to a boil and add the salt. Cook until the potatoes are completely tender, about 20 minutes. Drain and return them to the pot.

Mash the potatoes until smooth, or press through a ricer. Stir in the butter. When the butter is completely incorporated, stir in the hot milk and horseradish. Season with salt and pepper. Serve immediately or keep warm over hot water in a double boiler, uncovered, until ready to serve.

Garlic Mashed Potatoes

These potatoes are great with any meat dish but they go especially well with lamb. I like to make a meal of them accompanied by Red Swiss Chard with Bacon, Garlic and White Wine, page 132.

Makes about 4 cups (1 L)

2 lbs.	unpeeled red-skinned potatoes, scrubbed and cut into 1-inch (2.5-cm) cubes	900 g
2 tsp.	salt	10 ml
8	cloves roasted garlic, page 196	8
4 Tbsp.	unsalted butter	60 ml
1/2 cup	hot milk	125 ml
	salt and pepper to taste	

Place the potatoes in a large pot with enough cold water to cover them by 4 inches (10 cm). Bring to a boil and add the salt. Cook until the potatoes are completely tender, about 20 minutes. Drain and return them to the pot.

Mash the potatoes with the roasted garlic until smooth; stir in the butter. When the butter is completely incorporated, stir in the hot milk. Season with salt and pepper. Serve immediately or keep warm over hot water in a double boiler, uncovered, until ready to serve.

Potato and Rutabaga Cake

Serve this with Duck Breast with Rhubarb and Red Wine Sauce, page 96, or rack of lamb when you want to be extra fancy, or lamb leg when not in a fancy mood.

It is good on its own, with a dollop of sour cream or crème fraîche, page 192.

Serves 6

1 1/2 lbs.	peeled rutabagas	675 g
2 tsp.	salt	10 ml
1 1/2 lbs.	peeled potatoes	675 g
1 tsp.	coarsely ground black pepper	5 ml
3 Tbsp.	unsalted butter	45 ml
3 Tbsp.	vegetable oil	45 ml

Coarsely shred the rutabaga and toss with the salt. Put the rutabaga in a colander and place over a bowl. Weight and refrigerate overnight.

The next day, squeeze the rutabaga to remove any excess water. Place in a bowl. Coarsely shred the potatoes and squeeze out the water with your hands. Toss the potato with the rutabaga and pepper until evenly combined.

Heat the oven to 350°F (180°C). In a heat-proof, nonstick 12-inch (30-cm) skillet, heat 2 Tbsp. (30 ml) of the butter and 2 Tbsp. (30 ml) of the oil over medium-high heat. Press the potato and rutabaga mixture gently and evenly into the pan. Turn the heat to medium low and cook, checking frequently, until golden brown, about 10 minutes.

Flip the cake onto a plate, crisp side up. Add the remaining butter and oil to the pan. Slide the cake back into the pan and bake in the oven until golden brown on the bottom, about 10-15 minutes. Cut into wedges and serve. (The cake may be cooked up to 4 hours in advance. Place on a baking sheet and leave at room temperature. Before serving, heat in a 400°F (200°C) oven for 10-15 minutes until it is piping hot.)

Smothered Green Beans with Tomatoes and Basil

These beans can be served hot or cold as a salad. If you want to be cheeky, divide the recipe in half and use yellow tomatoes, purple basil and green beans for one half; and yellow beans, red tomatoes and green basil for the other half. Serve them side by side. Ooo la la!

Serves 4-6

1 lb.	ripe plum tomatoes, or a 28-oz. (796-ml) can plum tomatoes, well drained and coarsely chopped	450 g
4 Tbsp.	olive oil	60 ml
4	medium cloves garlic, minced	4
1 1/2 lbs.	green beans, topped and tailed	675 g
	salt and pepper	
1 cup	fresh basil leaves	250 ml

Peel the tomatoes if you are using fresh ones, and cut them into 1-inch (2.5-cm) pieces.

In a large pot, heat the olive oil over medium heat and sauté the garlic until it turns pale gold. Add the tomatoes and cook for a few minutes until the tomatoes soften. Stir in the green beans and season lightly with salt and pepper. Cover with a lid and cook, stirring occasionally, until the beans are tender but firm. If the tomatoes are still watery, turn up the heat and cook until the liquid evaporates. Stir in the basil just before serving.

Two Ways to Peel a Tomato

The first and more traditional method of peeling tomatoes is to score a small X on the bottom of each tomato and drop them into a pot of boiling water, a few at a time. After about 10 seconds, remove them with a slotted spoon and slip off the skins.

The second method is to use a swivel-headed vegetable peeler. This method is preferable for tomatoes that are going to be used raw. Starting at the top of the tomato, use the peeler in a back and forth motion to pare the skin away.

Cut the tomatoes in half and remove the seeds with a small spoon if you are using them raw, or squeeze the tomatoes, cut side downwards, if you are going to be cooking them.

Hoisin Baked Beans

These beans are more savory and spicy than the traditional, molasses-sweetened version. Chinese pork belly is a sweet cured bacon sold in pieces in Oriental grocery stores. Chinese sausage or regular bacon can be used instead.

Serves 6-8

3 cups	dried navy beans	750 ml
1 cup	finely diced onions	250 ml
4 cups	water	1 L
2/3 cup	ketchup	160 ml
1/2 cup	soya sauce	125 ml
1 Tbsp.	Dijon mustard	15 ml
3 Tbsp.	hoisin sauce*	45 ml
1 tsp.	chili paste*	5 ml
2	1/4-inch (.5-cm) slices ginger	2
6	cloves garlic, cut in half	6
1/4 lb.	cured Chinese pork belly or salt pork, diced (optional)	115 g

*Available at Oriental markets and well-stocked supermarkets.

Place the beans in a large pot and cover with 6 inches (15 cm) of water. Bring to a boil, then turn down to a simmer, skimming off the foam that rises to the top. Cook until the beans are tender. Drain.

Preheat the oven to 250°F (120°C). Combine the beans and remaining ingredients in a tall, narrow casserole dish with a tight-fitting lid. Cover and bake for 6 hours.

Glazed Carrots with Blackberry Vinegar and Basil

Serves 4

1 lb.	small carrots, peeled	450 g
2 Tbsp.	Blackberry Vinegar, page 192	30 ml
1 Tbsp.	brown sugar	15 ml
2 tsp.	unsalted butter	10 ml
	salt and pepper	
1 Tbsp.	coarsely chopped fresh basil	15 ml

Cut the carrots into long diagonals, 3/8 inch (1 cm) thick. Cook in rapidly boiling, lightly salted water until tender-crisp. Drain.

Combine the vinegar and brown sugar in a saucepan. Boil over high heat until reduced by half. Add the carrots, butter, salt and pepper. Toss until the butter has melted and the carrots are heated through. Stir in the basil and serve immediately.

Fiddleheads with Hazelnut Butter

When fiddleheads are in season I add them to pastas and salads as well as making this vegetable dish. I think their flavor and texture benefit from being cooked until very tender.

Serves 4-6

1 lb.	fiddleheads, trimmed and washed	450 g
2 Tbsp.	unsalted butter	30 ml
1	clove garlic, cut in half	1
2 Tbsp.	hazelnuts, roasted and finely chopped	30 ml
2 tsp.	lemon juice	10 ml
	salt to taste	

Bring a large pot of water to a boil. While waiting for the water to boil, melt the butter on medium heat and sauté the garlic until it turns golden. Remove and discard the garlic. Remove the pan from the heat and add the hazelnuts, lemon juice and salt.

Cook the fiddleheads in the pot of boiling water until they are completely tender. Drain well and toss with the hazelnut butter.

Blue Cheese and Spinach Tart

Serve as a main course with a tomato and basil salad or as an accompaniment to Seared Rabbit with Mustard and Fennel, page 108.

Serves 6

1/2 recipe	Savory Pastry, page 190	1/2 recipe
2	medium onions, peeled and thinly sliced	2
2 Tbsp.	unsalted butter	30 ml
1/4 lb.	spinach, stems removed	115 g
1/4 lb.	blue cheese, crumbled	115 g
3	large eggs	3
2 cups	half-and-half cream	500 ml
1/2 tsp.	salt	2.5 ml

Preheat oven to 400°F (200°C). Roll out the pastry and fit into an 8-inch (20-cm) tart pan with a removable bottom. Prick lightly with a fork and refrigerate for 15 minutes. Line with foil and fill with dried beans. Bake for 10 minutes. Remove the foil and beans and bake for 5 minutes longer. Remove from the oven and cool.

Sauté the onions in the butter until translucent. Set aside. Steam the spinach until just wilted. Cool, squeeze dry and finely chop. Scatter the onions, spinach and cheese over the bottom of the tart. Beat the eggs with the cream and salt. Pour into the tart. Bake for 15 minutes, then reduce the heat to 350°F (180°C) and bake for 20-25 minutes, or until just set. Allow to rest for 10 minutes before serving.

Red Swiss Chard with Bacon, Garlic and White Wine

This easy wintry dish will complement almost any simple meat or fish dish. You can substitute green Swiss chard, mustard greens or rapini for the red Swiss chard, if you like.

Serves 4

1 lb.	red Swiss chard, coarse stems removed, washed and drained	450 g
1 tsp.	vegetable oil	5 ml
2 slices	bacon, finely chopped	2 slices
2	cloves garlic, thinly sliced	2
1/3 cup	white wine	80 ml
1/8 tsp.	salt	.5 ml
	pepper to taste	

Coarsely chop the Swiss chard and reserve.

Heat the vegetable oil in a large pot over medium heat. Sauté the bacon and garlic until the bacon is crisp and the garlic is lightly browned. Add the Swiss chard, white wine and salt. Cover and cook over low heat until tender, approximately 10-12 minutes. Season with pepper just before serving.

Stir-Fried Watercress with Cherry Tomatoes

A speedy summer vegetable dish that is a good accompaniment to fish.

Serves 4-6

2 Tbsp.	vegetable oil	30 ml
3	medium cloves garlic, thinly sliced	3
1 Tbsp.	ginger, finely julienned	15 ml
2 cups	cherry tomatoes, stems removed	500 ml
2	large bunches watercress, coarse stems removed	2
	salt and pepper to taste	

Heat the vegetable oil in a wok or heavy skillet over high heat and stir-fry the garlic and ginger until the garlic turns pale gold. Add the cherry tomatoes and stir-fry for about a minute, until they glisten. Mix in the watercress and stir-fry until it wilts. Season to taste and serve immediately.

Herb and Spice Marinated Mushrooms

This may seem like a huge quantity of mushrooms, but they shrink drastically in the cooking. The mushrooms can be used as part of an antipasto plate, tossed in a salad, served as an accompaniment to barbecued steaks or sliced and mixed with grated cheese and melted on toasted bread.

Makes about 3 cups (750 ml)

1/2 cup	olive oil	125 ml
2 Tbsp.	red wine vinegar	30 ml
2 Tbsp.	lemon juice	30 ml
1 Tbsp.	ground coriander seeds	15 ml
2 tsp.	salt	10 ml
1 tsp.	coarsely ground black pepper	5 ml
2 1/2 lbs.	large, firm mushrooms	1 kg
2 tsp.	dried thyme	10 ml
1 Tbsp.	fennel seeds	15 ml
2	bay leaves	2
6	large cloves garlic, crushed	6
1 tsp.	coarsely chopped fresh marjoram leaves or 1/2 tsp. (2.5 ml) dried	5 ml
1 Tbsp.	finely chopped parsley	15 ml

In a large shallow pot mix the oil, vinegar, lemon juice, coriander, salt and pepper. Bring to a boil, add the mushrooms and simmer for 15 minutes until soft. Drain the mushrooms through a sieve, saving the liquid.

Place the thyme, fennel, bay leaves and garlic cloves in a piece of cheesecloth and tie securely. Place in a pot with the mushroom liquid. Boil hard for 5 minutes, or until most of the liquid evaporates. Place the drained mushrooms in a bowl and pour the hot liquid over them.

When the mushrooms are cool, add the marjoram and parsley.

The mushrooms keep well for 2 weeks, covered and refrigerated.

Miso-Marinated Shiitake Mushrooms

The fragrance and meaty texture of shiitake mushrooms have won the hearts of many. I like them simply prepared, as here. They are delicious on cooked asparagus, on an antipasto plate, beside roast chicken, in a spinach salad or sliced into hot cooked rice.

Serves 4-6

1 1/4 lbs.	fresh shiitake mushrooms	570 g
2 Tbsp.	light miso	30 ml
1 Tbsp.	sugar	15 ml
2 Tbsp.	toasted ground sesame seeds	30 ml
1/2 tsp.	sesame oil	2.5 ml
1 Tbsp.	soya sauce	15 ml

Bring 4 cups (1 L) of water to a boil. While waiting for the water to boil, cut the stems off the mushrooms.

Cook the mushrooms in the boiling water for 2 minutes, stirring constantly. Drain well, reserving 1 Tbsp. (15 ml) of the water.

Mix the miso thoroughly with the reserved water. Add the remaining ingredients and mix well. Squeeze the mushrooms between the palms of your hands to remove any water. Place in a bowl and mix well with the miso sauce. The mushrooms keep for a week, covered and refrigerated.

Beet and Apple Sauce

Serve this beautifully hued sauce wherever you would serve applesauce with a main dish.

Serves 4

2 Tbsp.	unsalted butter	30 ml
3/4 cup	finely diced onion	185 ml
1 1/2 cups	peeled and diced beets	375 ml
1 1/2 cups	apples, peeled, cored and thinly sliced	375 ml
1/2 tsp.	salt	2.5 ml
1/2 cup	water	125 ml
2 tsp.	cider vinegar	10 ml

Melt the butter in a saucepan over medium heat and sauté the onions until translucent. Add the beets, apples, salt and water. Cover tightly and simmer for about 30 minutes, until the beets are completely tender.

Transfer the beet mixture to a food processor and purée with the cider vinegar. Taste and adjust the seasoning. (The sauce may be prepared 1 day in advance. Cover and refrigerate. Reheat over low heat or in a microwave oven.)

Parsnip and Pear Purée

A delicious accompaniment to simple roast chicken and pork.

Serves 4-6

1 1/2 lbs.	parsnips	675 g
1	medium red-skinned potato, peeled and cut into 1-inch (2.5-cm) pieces	1
2	ripe Bartlett pears, peeled, cored and cut into 1-inch (2.5-cm) pieces	2
1	whole clove	1
	salt and pepper to taste	
2 Tbsp.	unsalted butter	30 ml
1 tsp.	good-quality balsamic vinegar	5 ml

Peel the parsnips, cut them into quarters and remove the woody cores. Cut the parsnips into 1-inch (2.5-cm) pieces. Cook the potatoes and parsnips in water to cover until they are tender. Drain.

While the potatoes and parsnips are cooking, simmer the pears and the clove in water until the pears are just tender but not mushy. Drain the pears and discard the clove.

Purée the vegetables and pears in the work bowl of a food processor or a food mill. Transfer to a saucepan and reheat gently. Season with salt and pepper. Stir in the butter and balsamic vinegar just before serving.

Sean's Millet, Apple and Blue Cheese Pilaf

Sean Brennan is a brilliant and inspirational chef who lives in Victoria. We have spent many hours talking and salivating over ideas together. Sean came up with this pilaf to accompany smoked black cod. Pork or venison would suit it as well. If you are not familiar with millet, this is a good place to start.

Serves 4

3/4 cup	millet	185 ml
1 1/2 cups	water	375 ml
1/2 tsp.	black mustard seeds	2.5 ml
2 Tbsp.	unsalted butter	30 ml
2/3 cup	finely diced onions	160 ml
1	apple, peeled, cored and diced into 1/4-inch (.5-cm) pieces	1
	salt and pepper to taste	
1/3 cup	blue cheese, crumbled	80 ml

Heat a heavy frying pan over medium heat. Stirring or shaking the pan constantly, roast the millet until it is flecked with brown spots. Transfer to a pot and add the water. Bring to a boil, cover and turn the heat to low. Cook for 40 minutes, until the millet is tender. Remove from the heat and fluff the millet with a fork. (The millet may be prepared up to one day ahead. Cool, cover and refrigerate.)

Heat a small frying pan over high heat. Dry-roast the black mustard seeds, shaking the pan constantly, until the seeds pop like a string of firecrackers. Transfer to a small bowl.

Melt the butter in a frying pan over medium heat. Sauté the onions and black mustard seeds until the onions are golden. Add the apple pieces and continue cooking until they are heated through but not soft. Add the millet and heat it through. Season with salt and pepper and stir in the blue cheese. Serve the pilaf as soon as the cheese starts to melt.

Bulgur Pilaf with Sage and Angel-Hair Pasta

This dish has a homey, satisfying texture and flavor. Try experimenting with the seasonings. Add some currants, dried apricots or raisins, if you like, or a few sprigs of lemon thyme or rosemary.

Serves 4-6

3 Tbsp.	vegetable oil	45 ml
2	cloves garlic, minced	2
2/3 cup	finely diced carrots	160 ml
2/3 cup	finely diced onion	160 ml
1/2 cup	finely diced celery	125 ml
1 1/2 cups	medium bulgur	375 ml
3 oz.	angel-hair pasta, a.k.a. cappelini, broken into 2-inch (5-cm) pieces	90 g
2 1/2 cups	water	625 ml
3/4 tsp.	salt	4 ml
2 tsp.	finely chopped fresh sage	10 ml
	freshly ground black pepper to taste	

Heat the vegetable oil in a saucepan over medium heat. Sauté the garlic, carrots, onion and celery until they are lightly browned. Add the bulgur and angel-hair pasta.

Sauté until the bulgur picks up white and light brown spots. Mix in the salted water, cover and cook over low heat for 20 minutes, until the water is absorbed and the bulgur is tender. Remove from the heat and stir in the sage and pepper.

Risotto

Nothing captures the essence of a vegetable like a well-made risotto. Fresh spring peas, beets, young carrots, squash, Swiss chard—all make excellent risotto.

The ingredients are quite humble—rice, fat, stock or water, vegetables, meat, fish and seasonings—but careful cooking creates something greater than any of these ingredients could be on their own.

It is important that a risotto be served hot and freshly cooked or it loses its creamy yet sinuous quality—the hallmark of a good risotto. (Of course, there is nothing wrong with eating it cold, straight out of the fridge, but that's the next *day.) Make it the focal point of your meal or serve it as a first course at a long and pleasant dinner.*

Someone once asked me what cooking was. I replied that it was alchemy. No, he said, it's heat and time. I considered this and decided that it was all three, especially when it comes to risotto.

Saffron Risotto

A great accompaniment to fish, especially the Alaskan Black Cod Ossobuco, page 78. Saffron is hand-gathered from crocuses. You may think it is expensive, but a little goes a long way. In fact, it is best to be prudent when using saffron. Too much will completely overwhelm a dish.

Serves 6

6 cups	chicken stock or water	1.5 L
1/4 cup	unsalted butter	60 ml
1/4 cup	finely diced onion	60 ml
2 cups	arborio rice*	500 ml
1/16 tsp.	saffron, steeped in 2 Tbsp. (30 ml) boiling water	.25 ml
	salt and pepper to taste	
1/4 cup	Parmesan cheese, grated	60 ml

*Available at Italian markets and well-stocked supermarkets.

Heat the stock or water to a simmer. Melt the butter in a large, heavy saucepan over medium heat and sauté the onion until translucent. Mix in the rice, stirring to coat with the butter and onions. Add a ladleful of stock and stir until the stock is absorbed and a loose, creamy film forms around the rice.

Continue adding the stock, one ladleful at a time, until the rice is half-cooked. Add half the saffron water and season with salt. Continue adding stock until the rice is tender but still firm to the bite. Add more saffron water if you feel that it is necessary and adjust the seasoning with salt and pepper. Stir in the Parmesan cheese and serve immediately.

Fava Bean, Asparagus and Pea Shoot Risotto

The inspiration for this risotto came from a late spring cruise through Chinatown, wondering what to have for dinner.

Serves 4-6

1 1/2 lbs.	fresh fava beans,* removed from their pods and peeled	675 g
8 cups	chicken stock or water	2 L
4 Tbsp.	unsalted butter	60 ml
1/2 cup	finely diced onions	125 ml
2 cups	arborio rice*	500 ml
	salt to taste	
1/2 lb.	fresh asparagus, trimmed and cut into 1-inch (2.5-cm) pieces on the diagonal	225 g
1 cup	fresh pea shoots,* packed	250 ml
	Parmesan cheese	
	salt and pepper to taste	

*Available at Italian markets and well-stocked supermarkets.

Bring a small pot of water to a boil. Add the fava beans and cook for 4-5 minutes until bright green. Drain and set aside.

Heat the stock or water to a simmer. Melt the butter over medium heat in a large pot and sauté the onions until translucent. Stir in the rice, coating it with the butter and onions. Add a ladleful of stock or water and stir until the liquid is absorbed and a loose, creamy film forms around the rice. Add the fava beans. Continue stirring in the stock, one ladleful at a time, until the rice is half-cooked. Season with the salt and add more stock until the rice is tender but still firm to the bite.

Five minutes before the risotto is done, add the asparagus. When the risotto is done, add the pea shoots and Parmesan cheese. Adjust the seasoning with salt and pepper. Serve immediately in heated bowls.

Fava Beans and Pea Shoots

Fava beans are also known as broad beans or Windsor beans. They have large, lumpy, bright green pods with a spongy interior enclosing the actual seed. The seeds must be removed from the pod and peeled before using. Look for fava beans that are bright, firm and without any brown spots on their pods. To me, their flavor can only be described as the essence of life. They are especially delicious with lamb.

Pea shoots are either the tender tips of the pea plant or the small leafy sprout grown from the seed. They can be stir-fried, tossed into salads, or added to soups at the last moment.

Butternut Squash Risotto

A beautiful, golden-colored risotto; the lemon zest punctuates its sweetness with bursts of flavor.

Serves 4-6

8 cups	chicken stock or water	2 L
4 Tbsp.	unsalted butter	60 ml
1/2 cup	finely diced onion	125 ml
2 cups	butternut squash, peeled and diced into 1/2-inch (1-cm) pieces	500 ml
2 cups	arborio rice*	500 ml
	salt and pepper to taste	
	zest of half a lemon	
1/2 cup	freshly grated Parmesan cheese	125 ml

*Available at Italian markets and well-stocked supermarkets.

Heat the stock or water to a simmer. Melt the butter over medium heat in a large pot and sauté the onions until translucent. Stir in the squash, coating it with the butter and onions. Add the rice and stir for a few minutes. Pour in a ladleful of stock or water and stir until the liquid is absorbed and a loose, creamy film forms around the rice.

Continue adding the stock, one ladleful at a time, until the rice is half-cooked. Season with salt. Continue adding stock until the rice is tender but still firm to the bite. Adjust the seasoning. Stir in the lemon zest and Parmesan cheese and serve immediately in heated bowls.

Desserts

Desserts

"What's for dessert?" I am sure I used to drive my mother crazy with that question. I always wanted to know what was for dinner too, but that was after I knew what dessert was. A hunk of roast beef, sizzling in the oven and emitting its unparalleled fatty aroma was far more obvious than her pineapple cream cake (no bake!), sitting discreetly, yet powerfully in the downstairs fridge.

A pastry chef is part of a special breed. They all have great handwriting. They are meticulous. They can coax fabulous, elegant and delicious creations out of simple ingredients. I love eating what they make, watching them work, and talking to them.

I am not a pastry chef and do not pretend to be. A dessert that I make has to be easy, quick and delicious. In my twenties, I went through a period of making Gâteau St. Honore, Dacquoise, Marjolaines and all those other masterpieces of French pastry. Nowadays, if I am feeling especially ambitious, I might toss off a Dobostorte for my husband's birthday. And I do bake Christmas cookies like a maniac, in the spirit of my mother, to give away as Christmas gifts.

I am content to nibble on a piece of good Belgian chocolate and a few walnuts and call that dessert. Or eat not one, but two flavors of ice cream from the same bowl. But there has *to be dessert.*

My birthday cake for the last six years has been the chocolate and whipped cream cake on the box of Nabisco Chocolate Wafers. It is fast, non-threatening (in case anyone would want to make it for me), and requires no special skill. Most of the recipes in this section fall into this category.

Plum and Toasted Almond Tart

The final flavor of the tart depends on the flavor of the plums. Choose plums that have a perfect balance of sweet and sour. Too-sweet plums will make a blah tart.

Makes 1 9-inch (22-cm) tart, serving 6-8

Almond Filling

1 cup	sliced almonds, lightly toasted	250 ml
2 Tbsp.	all-purpose flour	30 ml
1/2 cup	unsalted butter, cut into small pieces	125 ml
1/3 cup	sugar	80 ml
1	large egg	1
1/4 tsp.	almond extract	1.2 ml

Combine the almonds and flour in a food processor and pulse until finely ground but not oily.

Cream the butter and sugar until smooth and fluffy. Beat in the egg. Add the almonds and almond extract and beat until smooth and light, scraping down the sides of the bowl occasionally. (The filling may be made up to 2 days ahead. Cover and refrigerate.)

Crust

3 cups	all-purpose flour	750 ml
3/4 cups	icing sugar	185 ml
1/2 cup	sliced almonds	125 ml
3/4 cup	cold unsalted butter, cut into 1/2-inch (1-cm) cubes	185 ml

Pulse the flour, sugar and almonds in a food processor until finely ground. Scatter the butter over the top and pulse until the mixture crumbles. Pour out onto a flat surface and knead lightly until the dough holds together. Wrap in plastic wrap and chill for at least 2 hours or up to 2 days. Let the dough come to room temperature before using.

Preheat the oven to 400°F (200°C). Press the dough evenly into a 9-inch (22-cm) tart ring with a removable bottom. Thoroughly prick the shell with a fork. Weight the shell (see Savory Pastry, page 190) and bake for 15 minutes. Remove the weight, lower the oven temperature to 350°F (180°C) and bake for another 15-20 minutes until pale gold. Remove from the oven and cool.

To Assemble the Tart

8	ripe plums, cut in half and pitted	8

Preheat the oven to 350°F (180°C). Pour the almond filling into the crust. Push the plum halves, skin side up, halfway into the filling. Bake for 35-40 minutes until the filling is golden brown and slightly puffed. Remove from the oven and cool on a wire rack. Serve with lightly sweetened whipping cream or Crème Fraîche, page 192.

Upside-Down Pear Tart

I think this is my favorite of all winter desserts. For best flavor and texture, serve it warm or at room temperature.

Makes 1 10-inch (25-cm) tart, serving 6-8

2 cups	all-purpose flour	500 ml
1 Tbsp.	sugar	15 ml
1/4 tsp.	salt	1.2 ml
3/4 cup	unsalted butter, well chilled	185 ml
1/3 cup	ice-cold water	80 ml
8	slightly under-ripe Bartlett pears	8
1/2 cup	unsalted butter	125 ml
1 cup	sugar	250 ml

Place the flour, the 1 Tbsp. (15 ml) sugar and salt in a large bowl and whisk well to combine. Cut the 3/4 cup (185 ml) butter into 1/4-inch (.5-cm) cubes and toss with the flour mixture. Add the water all at once and blend it in with your hand. Knead gently with the tips of your fingers until the dough forms a rough ball. There will be dots of butter here and there through the dough. Flatten the dough and wrap in plastic wrap. Refrigerate for 1/2 hour.

Preheat the oven to 400°F (200°C). While the pastry is chilling, peel, core and cut the pears into quarters. Have a deep 10-inch (25-cm) pie plate at hand. In a heavy frying pan melt the 1/2 cup (125 ml) butter over medium heat. Add the 1 cup (250 ml) sugar and cook, stirring frequently, until the sugar turns a deep brown. Add the pears and cook them, turning frequently. As the pears cook, they will shrink considerably and exude juice that will combine with the sugar and butter to form a syrup. Each piece of pear will become caramelized all the way through. As this happens, transfer the pieces, cut side down, to the pie plate. When all the pears are done, pour the syrup and any remaining pears into the pie pan.

On a floured surface, roll the pastry out to 1/4-inch (.5-cm) thickness. Cut a circle out of the pastry that is 1 inch (2.5 cm) larger than the top of the pie pan. Roll the pastry around the rolling pin and unroll it over the pears. Lightly tuck the edges into the pan. Place in the oven and bake for 20-30 minutes, until the pastry is golden brown. Allow the tart to cool to warm before turning it out onto a plate.

Serve with lightly whipped cream or Crème Fraîche, page 192.

The tart is best served warm on the same day it was made. If you wish, you may bake it in advance and reheat it in a low oven.

Blueberry and Cream Cheese Tart

Raspberries or blackberries are fabulous with this tart, too. For a really special treat, use the Chocolate Pastry, page 172, and raspberries as the topping.

Serves 8

1/2 cup	cream cheese	125 ml
1/4 cup	sugar	60 ml
1/2 tsp.	lemon zest, grated	2.5 ml
1/4 cup	whipping cream	60 ml
1	9-inch (22-cm) Sweet Shortcrust tart shell, page 189, fully baked	1
1 1/2 cups	blueberries	375 ml

In a mixing bowl, whisk together the cream cheese, sugar and lemon zest. In a separate bowl, whip the cream into soft peaks. Gently fold the cream into the cream cheese mixture.

Spread the cream cheese mixture evenly over the bottom of the pie shell. Place an even layer of blueberries over the top. Refrigerate for at least one hour to set the cheese. This tart loses its charm if it sits for too long, so serve it on the same day it is made.

Raspberry and Lemon Cream Cheese Tart

A refreshing summer dessert that can be made with any berries in season.

Makes 1 10-inch (25-cm) tart, serving 8

1/2 cup	lemon juice	125 ml
1 Tbsp.	gelatine	15 ml
6	large egg yolks	6
1 cup	sugar	250 ml
1 lb.	cream cheese	450 g
1/2 cup	unsalted butter	125 ml
2 Tbsp.	lemon zest, finely grated	30 ml
4	egg whites	4
1 pt.	raspberries	500 ml
1 recipe	Sweet Shortcrust Pastry, page 189, fully baked	1 recipe

Combine the lemon juice and gelatine. Let stand until the gelatine softens. Beat the egg yolks with a mixer or by hand until thick. Gradually beat in the sugar until thick and lemon-colored. Place in a heavy saucepan with the gelatine and cook over medium-low heat until the mixture lightly coats the back of a spoon. Pour into a bowl.

Beat the cream cheese and unsalted butter by hand or with an electric mixer until smooth. Gradually beat in the lemon zest and custard mixture. Chill until cool, stirring occasionally.

Beat the egg whites until soft peaks form. Fold into the cooled cream cheese mixture. Pour into the baked pie shell and chill until firm, about 3 hours.

Place the raspberries on top of the tart in any way that pleases you. Serve the same day.

Apple and Raspberry Pie

A toothsome combination!

Makes 1 9-inch (22-cm) pie

2 recipes	Sweet Shortcrust Pastry, page 189	2 recipes
8	apples, peeled, cored and cut into 1/3-inch (.8-cm) slices	8
3/4 cup	light brown sugar	185 ml
4 Tbsp.	flour	60 ml
1 tsp.	cinnamon	5 ml
2 pts.	raspberries	1 L
2 Tbsp.	unsalted butter	30 ml
1	egg	1
1 Tbsp.	water	15 ml
2 tsp.	sugar	10 ml

Chill the pastry, then cut it in half, making one piece slightly larger than the other. Roll out the larger piece into an 11-inch (28-cm) circle and carefully fit into the bottom of the pie pan, leaving a 1-inch (2.5-cm) overhang all around. Roll out the other half into a 10-inch (25-cm) circle and place it on a baking sheet. Refrigerate both.

Preheat the oven to 375°F (190°). Place the apple slices in a large bowl and toss well with the sugar, flour and cinnamon. Add the raspberries and toss gently. Place the mixture in the pastry-lined pie pan, mounding it slightly. Dot with the butter. Place the top crust over the pie. Trim the edges and crimp the pastry. Beat the egg and water together and brush the top and edges of the pie with it. Sprinkle with the sugar.

Bake for 40-50 minutes until the juices are thick and bubbling and the crust is a deep golden brown. Cool completely before cutting.

Peach and Raspberry Crumble

My mother made an especially good crumble topping. It was so good that my sisters and I once ate all the topping from one, picking off the crunchy chunks one by one as it sat cooling on the counter. We became so involved in what we were doing that we didn't notice we were completely demolishing the top. When we realized what we had done, we silently dispersed, hoping naively that it wouldn't be noticed. It was noticed, of course, but I still take pleasure in picking chunks from the top of a crumble.

Serves 4-6

6	ripe, juicy peaches	6
1/4 cup	sugar	60 ml
3 Tbsp.	flour	45 ml
1/2 tsp.	cinnamon	2.5 ml
1/4 tsp.	ground dried ginger	1.2 ml
2 pts.	fresh raspberries	1 L
3/4 cup	flour	185 ml
1/4 tsp.	salt	1.2 ml
1/2 tsp.	baking powder	2.5 ml
3/4 cup	light brown sugar	185 ml
3/4 cup	chilled, unsalted butter	185 ml
1 1/2 cups	old-fashioned rolled oats	375 ml

Preheat the oven to 350°F (180°C). Peel the peaches, cut them in half and remove the pit. Cut each half into four wedges and place in a bowl. Add the sugar, 3 Tbsp. (45 ml) flour, cinnamon and ginger and toss well. Add the raspberries and toss gently. Transfer to a shallow, 2-quart (2-L) baking dish.

In a large bowl, whisk the 3/4 cup (185 ml) flour, salt and baking powder together. Whisk in the brown sugar. Cut the butter into 1-inch (2.5-cm) cubes and add to the flour mixture. Work the butter in with your fingertips until crumbly. Add the oats and gently work them into the mixture. Spread evenly and loosely over the fruit. Bake for 30-40 minutes until the topping is golden brown and the fruit bubbles up around the edges.

Blueberry and Apple Bread Pudding

I think bread pudding was the first baked dessert I ever made. It all seemed so complicated at the time. I was filled with a sense of wonder upon removing it from the oven. To my nine-year-old self, this gloriously golden, creamy puff of a thing seemed like a miracle. I couldn't resist digging into the puddles of custard between the bread while waiting for it to cool.

Stale croissants, egg bread or brioche instead of plain white bread make a marvellous bread pudding. You can also use marion-berries or raspberries instead of blueberries.

Serves 6-8

1	loaf of good white bread, about 24 oz. (675 g)	1
2 cups	blueberries	500 ml
2	apples, peeled, cored and diced	2
1 tsp.	cinnamon	5 ml
1/2 cup	unsalted butter, melted	125 ml
4	large eggs	4
3	large egg yolks	3
3/4 cup	sugar	185 ml
2 cups	half-and-half cream	500 ml
2 cups	milk	500 ml
1 Tbsp.	pure vanilla extract	15 ml
1/2 tsp.	nutmeg	2.5 ml
1/2 tsp.	cinnamon	2.5 ml
1/4 cup	sugar	60 ml

Trim the crusts off the bread and cut into 1-inch (2.5-cm) cubes. Toss gently in a large bowl with the blueberries, apples, 1 tsp. (5 ml) cinnamon and melted butter. Transfer the mixture to a lightly buttered 2-qt. (2-L) baking dish. Beat the eggs, egg yolks and 3/4 cup (185 ml) sugar together. Beat in the cream, milk and vanilla. Pour over the bread mixture and let sit for 1 hour.

Preheat the oven to 350°F (180°C). Place the baking dish in a larger baking pan and and pour in hot water to come halfway up the sides of the baking dish. Combine the nutmeg, cinnamon and 1/4 cup (60 ml) sugar and sprinkle over the pudding. Bake until the pudding is golden brown, about 1 hour. Remove from the oven and let the pudding cool in the water bath. As the pudding is cooling, use a very small spoon to dig trenches out of the custard. Invite others to do the same. Serve at room temperature with lightly whipped cream.

Carmen's Warm Persimmon Pudding

This warm pudding is a luscious late fall dessert. If you have never had persimmons before, this is a good way to start. The really ripe and fragrant ones you need for this recipe are generally less expensive than the perfect glowing orange ones available for sale in the fall.

Makes 1 9-inch (22-cm) tart, serving 6-8

4	large, very soft persimmons	4
3	large eggs	3
1 cup	sugar	250 ml
1/2 cup	unsalted butter, melted	125 ml
1 1/2 cups	flour	375 ml
1 tsp.	baking soda	5 ml
1 tsp.	baking powder	5 ml
1/2 tsp.	ground ginger	2.5 ml
1/2 tsp.	ground cinnamon	2.5 ml
1/4 tsp.	ground allspice	1.2 ml
1/2 tsp.	salt	2.5 ml
2 cups	half-and-half cream	500 ml

Preheat the oven to 350°F (180°C). Butter an 8-inch (20-cm) springform pan.

To make the persimmon purée, cut the persimmons in half and scoop out the pulp. Press through a sieve and discard the seeds and fibers. You should have 2 cups (500 ml) of purée. (To quickly ripen persimmons, freeze them overnight. They will be ready to use when thawed completely.)

With a mixer or by hand, beat the eggs and sugar until well combined. Beat in the melted butter.

Sift the dry ingredients together and stir into the egg mixture. Stir in the cream, then the persimmon purée. Pour into the oiled pan and bake for about 40 minutes, or until a skewer inserted in the middle comes out clean. The pudding will sink as it cools. Serve warm with lightly whipped cream if desired.

Aunt Toni's Steamed Cranberry Pudding with Eggnog Sauce

For years Uncle Leo took all the credit for our family's traditional Christmas dessert. Finally, the truth can be told!

It is well worth investing in a pudding mold to make this once-a-year treat. It has a perfect, mouthwatering, sweet and sour flavor that is hard to resist—even when you are stuffed with turkey.

Serves 8

6 Tbsp.	unsalted butter	90 ml
3/4 cup	sugar	185 ml
2	large eggs	2
2 1/4 cups	flour	560 ml
2 1/2 tsp.	baking powder	12.5 ml
1/4 tsp.	salt	1.2 ml
1/2 cup	milk	125 ml
2 cups	cranberries, fresh or frozen	500 ml
1/2 cup	walnuts or hazelnuts, coarsely chopped	125 ml

Eggnog Sauce

1 cup	unsalted butter	250 ml
1/2 cup	sugar	125 ml
2 cups	prepared eggnog	500 ml
1/2 cup	rum or brandy	125 ml

Butter and flour the inside and lid of a 6-cup (1.5 L) pudding mold. Set aside.

Cream the butter and sugar until light and fluffy. Add the eggs one at a time, beating well after each addition. Sift the dry ingredients together. Add to the butter mixture alternately with the milk. Fold in the cranberries and nuts and pack into the prepared mold. Place the mold in a pot and pour boiling water into the pot to reach halfway up the side of the mold. Cover with a lid and simmer gently for 2 hours, replenishing with boiling water as necessary.

Remove the pudding from the pot, uncover and cool for 15 minutes before removing from the mold. (The pudding may be wrapped securely in foil and frozen for up to a month. Thaw and resteam for 15 minutes before serving.)

To make the eggnog sauce, combine the butter, sugar and eggnog in a heavy pot. Bring to a boil and cook for 5 minutes, stirring constantly. Remove from the heat. Stir in the rum or brandy.

Cut the warm pudding into slices and pass the sauce separately.

Summer Pudding

One of the glories of summer occurs when raspberries and currants are ripe and ready to be made into this dessert. It is so mouth-watering and easy to make that it deserves to be more popular. Bread and stewed fruit do not provoke the imagination or taste buds, but sitting overnight together transforms these simple ingredients into an exquisite dessert.

Local food writer Noël Richardson said that summer pudding was made with gooseberries on Saturna Island, where she grew up, and was called Saturna Pudding. Saturna is such a romantic, even magical-sounding name. Next summer I'll be sure to make it with gooseberries.

Serves 6-8

1	large loaf unsliced white bread, one or two days old	1
2 cups	red or white currants, stems removed	500 ml
1 cup	granulated sugar	250 ml
3 Tbsp.	water	45 ml
2 1/2 pts.	raspberries (save a few for garnish)	1.2 L
	lightly sweetened whipped cream or Crème Fraîche, page 192	

Select a bowl of 2-quart (2-L) capacity in which to make the pudding. Line it with plastic wrap.

Cut the crusts from the bread and cut into 3/4-inch (2-cm) slices. Cut each slice diagonally. Line the bowl with the bread so that there are no gaps.

Combine the currants, sugar and water in a saucepan and cook over medium heat, stirring gently from time to time, until the currants start to release their juice. Add the raspberries and cook until their juice starts to run. Pour into the bread-lined mold and cover with a layer of bread. Bring the plastic wrap up over the top of the pudding, using more plastic wrap if needed to cover the top. Place a plate of about the same diameter as the bowl on top of the pudding and weight it down with a few cans or jars. Refrigerate overnight. (The pudding may be made up to 3 days in advance.)

To serve, remove the weights and plates from the pudding and open the plastic wrap. Invert the pudding onto a plate and remove the plastic wrap. Garnish with the mint sprigs and reserved raspberries. Pass a bowl of whipped cream or crème fraîche separately.

Aldergrove Sour Cherry Upside-Down Cake

We have an ancient sour cherry tree in the backyard that produces about 14 cherries each season. Every year a determined swarm of black birds descends upon the tree and pecks the few cherries to pulp. Since I have no interest in tree pruning or bird shooing, the easier alternative is driving to Aldergrove and picking the cherries. They end up in Sour and Sweet Cherry Ketchup, page 195, and this delicious cake.

Makes 1 9-inch (22-cm) cake

1 cup	brown sugar	250 ml
1/2 cup	walnut halves	125 ml
3/4 lb.	fresh sour cherries, pitted	350 g
1/2 cup	unsalted butter	125 ml
2	drops almond extract	2
2	large eggs	2
2/3 cup	granulated sugar	160 ml
1 tsp.	pure vanilla extract	5 ml
6 Tbsp.	milk	90 ml
1 cup	all-purpose flour	250 ml
1/2 tsp.	baking powder	2.5 ml
1/4 tsp.	salt	1.2 ml

Preheat the oven to 350°F (180°C). Butter the sides of a round 9-inch (22-cm) baking pan.

Distribute the brown sugar evenly over the bottom of the pan. Sprinkle the walnuts over the sugar and then the cherries. Melt the butter and stir in the almond extract. Pour evenly over the cherries.

With an electric mixer or by hand, beat the eggs until foamy. Gradually beat in the granulated sugar until light. Beat in the vanilla and milk. Sift the dry ingredients together and mix into the eggs, stirring only until combined. Spread evenly over the cherries. Bake for 25-30 minutes, until the top springs back when lightly pressed. Remove from the oven and cool on a rack for 10 minutes. Run a knife around the edge and turn out onto a plate. Serve with lightly whipped cream, if you wish.

Plum and Toasted Almond Upside-Down Cake

A backyard inspiration. What do you do with a treeful of delicious plums? Well, you could make jam, or plum sauce or a cake. I would take the cake over anything else.

Makes 1 9-inch (22-cm) cake

1 cup	brown sugar	250 ml
1/2 cup	unblanched almonds, roasted and coarsely chopped	125 ml
8	sour plums, cut in half and pitted	8
1/2 cup	unsalted butter	125 ml
2	large eggs	2
2/3 cup	granulated sugar	160 ml
1 tsp.	pure vanilla extract	5 ml
6 Tbsp.	milk	90 ml
1 cup	all-purpose flour	250 ml
1/2 tsp.	baking powder	2.5 ml
1/4 tsp.	salt	1.2 ml

Preheat the oven to 350°F (180°C). Butter the sides of a round 9-inch (22-cm) baking pan.

Distribute the brown sugar evenly over the bottom of the pan. Sprinkle the almonds over the sugar and then the pitted plums, skin side down. Melt the butter and pour evenly over the plums.

With an electric mixer or by hand, beat the eggs until foamy. Gradually beat in the granulated sugar until light. Beat in the vanilla and milk. Sift the dry ingredients together and mix into the egg mixture, stirring only until combined. Spread evenly over the plums. Bake for 25-30 minutes until the top springs back when lightly pressed.

Remove from the oven and cool on a rack for 10 minutes. Run a knife around the edge and turn out onto a plate. Serve with lightly whipped cream, if desired.

Strawberry Shortcake

One of the ultimate summer pleasures. One of my favorite things about it, besides eating it, is squashing the berries with my hands and watching them flow between my fingers. It is a very satisfying activity.

Serves 8

2 1/4 cups	flour	560 ml
1/2 cup	sugar	125 ml
1 1/2 tsp.	baking powder	7.5 ml
3/4 tsp.	baking soda	4 ml
1/2 tsp.	salt	2.5 ml
6 Tbsp.	unsalted butter, chilled	90 ml
2/3 cup	buttermilk	160 ml
1	large egg yolk	1
1/2 tsp.	vanilla extract	2.5 ml
3 pts.	strawberries, washed and hulled	1.5 L
1/4 cup	sugar	60 ml
3 cups	whipping cream	750 ml
2 Tbsp.	sugar	30 ml

Preheat the oven to 350°F (180°C). Sift the flour, sugar, baking powder, baking soda and salt into a large bowl. Cut the butter into 1/2-inch (1-cm) cubes and toss with the flour mixture. Cut in the butter with a pastry blender or two knives until mealy. Beat the buttermilk, egg yolk and vanilla together. Combine the buttermilk with the flour mixture, stirring with a fork until just combined. Transfer the dough to a buttered and floured baking sheet and pat out evenly into a 9-inch (22-cm) circle. Bake for 15-20 minutes until golden brown. Transfer to a rack to cool.

Slice 2 cups (500 ml) of the strawberries and reserve. Lightly mash the remaining berries with a potato masher (or your hands). Stir in the sugar and set aside until you are ready to assemble the shortcake.

When the shortcake is completely cool, split it in half horizontally. Whip the cream with the sugar into soft peaks. Spread half of the mashed berries on the bottom half of the shortcake. Cover with half of the whipped cream. Gently cover with the top half of the shortcake. Spread the remaining berries and whipped cream on the top. Decorate with the reserved sliced berries. Refrigerate for at least 1/2 hour before serving.

Sour Dried Cherry and Chocolate Pound Cake

The inspiration for this cake came from two sources—sampling chocolate-covered cherries from a well-known West Coast coffee purveyor and wondering what to do with some delicious dried sour cherries. They both had intense flavors, just begging to be captured in a cake. You may use any chocolate-covered cherry that strikes your fancy as long as it is not gooey. I gave this away as Christmas cake and the crowd went wild. If you can resist temptation, the cake keeps for 4 weeks, wrapped and refrigerated.

Makes 1 10-inch (25-cm) tube pan, about 20 slices

3/4 lb.	dried sour cherries	350 g
1 cup	bourbon	250 ml
2 cups	all-purpose flour	500 ml
1 tsp.	baking powder	5 ml
1/2 tsp.	salt	2.5 ml
1 cup	unsalted butter	250 ml
2 cups	granulated sugar	500 ml
6	large eggs, separated	6
1/2 lb.	chocolate-covered cherries, cut in half	225 g
1/4 lb.	finely chopped bittersweet chocolate	115 g
1 lb.	walnut halves	450 g

A day before baking the cake, combine the sour cherries and bourbon in a small saucepan. Bring to a simmer and remove from the heat. Transfer to a bowl, cool and cover. (The cherries may be prepared up to 5 days in advance. Keep tightly covered.)

Preheat the oven to 275°F (135°C). Generously butter a 10- by 4-inch (25- by 10-cm) tube pan. Line the bottom with parchment paper and butter the paper. Dust the pan with flour and shake out the excess.

Sift the flour, baking powder and 1/4 tsp. (1.2 ml) of the salt together. In a large bowl, cream the butter with an electric mixer until light. Gradually incorporate 1 3/4 cups (440 ml) of the sugar, beating for 5 minutes until creamy. Beat in the egg yolks. On low speed beat in a third of the flour mixture, then half the cherries and bourbon, then another third of the flour mixture, the rest of the cherries and bourbon, and the remaining flour. Beat only until the ingredients are incorporated after each addition, as over-beating will make the cake tough. Stir in the chocolate-covered cherries, chocolate and walnuts.

Using clean beaters, beat the egg whites with the reserved 1/4 tsp. (1.2 ml) salt until the whites form a soft shape. Gradually add the reserved 1/4 cup (60 ml) sugar and beat to soft peaks.

Stir a quarter of the egg whites into the batter, then fold in the rest. Turn the batter into the prepared pan and smooth the top. Bake on the middle shelf for 2 1/2 hours, until a cake tester comes out clean. Remove from the oven and cool on a rack for 30 minutes.

Carefully run a knife around the sides of the pan and turn the cake out onto a rack. Remove the parchment paper and cool completely. Wrap the cake in plastic wrap and age it for at least a day before serving.

Yogurt Cheese with Fresh Strawberries

A light and easy summer dessert.

Serves 6

2 1/2 cups	plain, Balkan-style yogurt	625 ml
6 Tbsp.	fragrant honey	90 ml
2 pts.	fresh strawberries	1 L

Whisk the yogurt and honey in a bowl until thoroughly combined. Either line a *coeur à la crème* mold or a small basket with cheesecloth (see Ethereal Chocolate Cream, page 173). Pour the yogurt mixture into the mold and fold the excess cheesecloth over the top. Place on a plate or over a bowl to catch the drips. Cover the top with plastic wrap. Cut a small piece of cardboard to fit on top of the mold. Place on top of the yogurt and place a weight on top. A small can would do nicely. Refrigerate overnight.

When ready to serve, open the top of the cheesecloth and turn the yogurt out onto a plate. Remove the cheesecloth. Hull and cut the berries in half if they are small; quarters if larger. Slice the yogurt cheese into wedges and serve with the strawberries.

Fresh Ginger and Buttermilk Cake

Besides being mouth-warming, this super-moist ginger cake has a heart-warming flavor. Eat it with butter while looking out the window on a rainy day.

Makes 1 10-inch (25-cm) cake, serving 8-10

3/4 cup	unsalted butter, softened	185 ml
1/2 cup	brown sugar	125 ml
2	eggs	2
1 cup	molasses	250 ml
3 Tbsp.	finely grated fresh ginger	45 ml
3 Tbsp.	finely chopped crystallized ginger	45 ml
1 cup	all-purpose flour	250 ml
1 cup	whole-wheat pastry flour	250 ml
2 tsp.	baking soda	10 ml
1 tsp.	ground dried ginger	5 ml
1 cup	buttermilk or yogurt	250 ml

Preheat the oven to 350°F (180°C). Butter and flour a 10-inch (25-cm) springform pan.

Cream the butter and sugar until light and fluffy. Beat in the eggs one at a time, then the molasses, fresh ginger and crystallized ginger. The mixture will look curdled. Sift the flours, baking soda and dried ginger together. Fold the dry ingredients and the buttermilk alternately into the butter mixture, a third at a time.

Pour the batter into the prepared pan. Bake in the center of the preheated oven for about 50 minutes, or until a cake tester comes out clean. Cool on a rack for 10 minutes before turning it out of the pan. Allow to cool completely before cutting. The cake will fall a bit in the center and this is how it should be.

You can serve this cake as is, or with a bowl of Rhubarb Compote (page 167) on the side to dunk your piece of cake into. Or, go all out and serve it with Crème Fraîche (page 192) *and* rhubarb compote.

Pumpkin Cheesecake

Better than pumpkin pie. Serve it for Thanksgiving this year.

Makes 1 8-inch (20-cm) cheesecake

1 1/4 cups	graham wafer crumbs	310 ml
1/2 tsp.	dried ground ginger	2.5 ml
1/4 tsp.	cinnamon	1.2 ml
1/4 cup	unsalted butter, melted	60 ml
1 Tbsp.	molasses	15 ml
1 3/4 lbs.	cream cheese	800 g
1/2	25-oz. (750-ml) can pumpkin purée	1/2
3/4 cup	brown sugar, packed	185 ml
4	large eggs	4
1/2 tsp.	dried ground ginger	2.5 ml
1/4 tsp.	ground allspice	1.2 ml
3/4 tsp.	ground cinnamon	4 ml
1/4 tsp.	freshly grated nutmeg	1.2 ml
2 Tbsp.	molasses	30 ml

To make the crust, combine the graham wafer crumbs, ginger and cinnamon and mix well. Combine the molasses and melted butter and stir well. Mix thoroughly with the dry ingredients. Press into the bottom of an 8-inch (20-cm) springform pan.

In a food processor, combine the remaining ingredients. Blend, scraping down the sides of the bowl occasionally until smooth. Pour into the prepared pan. Bake at 350°F (180°C) for 30-45 minutes until the cake is barely jiggly in the center. Remove from the oven and cool to room temperature. Refrigerate overnight before serving.

Candied Cranberry Cheesecake

Better than cherry cheesecake.

Makes 1 8-inch (20-cm) cheesecake

3 cups	granulated sugar	750 ml
3/4 lb.	fresh or frozen cranberries	350 g
1 1/2 cups	graham wafer crumbs	375 ml
1/2 tsp.	ground cinnamon	2.5 ml
1/2 cup	unsalted butter, melted	125 ml
2 lbs.	cream cheese	900 g
1 cup	granulated sugar	250 ml
4	large eggs	4
1 1/2 cups	sour cream	375 ml
2 Tbsp.	granulated sugar	30 ml
1 tsp.	pure vanilla extract	5 ml

One day before you plan to make the cheesecake, combine the 3 cups (750 ml) sugar and 3 cups (750) water in a saucepan and bring to a boil. Turn down to a simmer and add the cranberries. Cook just until they pop. Remove from the heat. Cool, cover and refrigerate overnight. (The cranberries may be prepared up to one month in advance.)

One hour before making the cheesecake, drain the cranberries in a sieve over a bowl to catch the syrup. Reserve the syrup.

Preheat the oven to 350°F (180°C). Lightly butter the inside of an 8-inch (20-cm) springform pan. Combine the graham wafer crumbs, cinnamon and melted butter. Mix thoroughly and press into the bottom of the pan. Set aside.

Cream the cream cheese, then beat in the 1 cup (250 ml) sugar. Add the eggs, one at a time, beating only until each egg is incorporated. By hand, fold in the cranberries. Pour into the prepared pan and bake for 30-45 minutes. The center of the cake should still jiggle a bit.

While the cake is baking, mix the sour cream, 2 Tbsp. (30 ml) sugar and vanilla together. Spread the sour cream mixture over the top. Return to the oven for 5 minutes. Cool the cheesecake completely and refrigerate overnight.

Serve the cheesecake with a pool of the cranberry syrup.

Caramelized Apple Cheesecake

An unusual and delicious topping for cheesecake. Try it in the fall when apples are at their best.

Makes 1 9-inch (22-cm) cake

1/2 cup	unsalted butter, melted	125 ml
1/2 tsp.	ground cinnamon	2.5 ml
1 1/2 cups	graham wafer crumbs	375 ml
1 1/2 lbs.	cream cheese	675 g
2/3 cup	sugar	160 ml
3	eggs	3
1/2 tsp.	vanilla	2.5 ml
6	medium, tart apples, peeled and cored	6
2 Tbsp.	unsalted butter	30 ml
1/2 cup	sugar	125 ml

Preheat the oven to 300°F (150°C).

To make the crust, combine the melted butter, cinnamon and graham wafer crumbs. Press into the bottom of a 9-inch (22-cm) springform pan.

For the filling, cream the cream cheese either by hand or with an electric mixer. Beat in the sugar. Add the eggs one at a time, beating well after each. Mix in the vanilla. Pour the mixture into the crust and bake for 45-50 minutes, until just set.

While the cheesecake is baking, make the apple topping. Cut the apples into 1/4-inch (.5-cm) slices. Melt the butter in a heavy frying pan over medium heat. Add the sugar and cook, stirring occasionally, until the sugar turns nut brown. Add the apple slices and turn the heat to low. Cover the pan and cook until the apples are tender, about 15 minutes. Uncover the pan and cook over high heat until the juice is thick and syrupy, stirring occasionally.

When the cheesecake has cooled to room temperature, spread the cooled apple mixture over the top. Refrigerate overnight before serving.

Crème Fraîche, Basil and Honey Mousse with Cinnamon-Poached Strawberries

You may have a puzzled look on your face after reading this recipe title. Basil is usually associated with savory dishes, but its flavor works extremely well with creamy desserts, such as ice cream or crème anglaise, and with sweet spices like cinnamon, ginger and nutmeg. Try it and see!

Serves 4

2 cups	Crème Fraîche, page 192	500 ml
2 Tbsp.	fragrant honey	30 ml
1 Tbsp.	icing sugar	15 ml
1 Tbsp.	finely chopped basil leaves	15 ml
1/4 cup	sugar	60 ml
1 1/2 cups	water	375 ml
1	4-inch (10-cm) piece cinnamon stick, broken into pieces	1
2 pts.	strawberries	1 L
	basil sprigs for garnish	

Line 4 5- to 6-oz. (150- to 180-g) ramekins with 4 layers of cheesecloth. Let enough of the cheesecloth hang over the edge to be able to fold it over the top when the ramekin is filled.

Whip the crème fraîche, honey and icing sugar with a whisk until it forms soft peaks. Stir in the basil. Divide evenly among the 4 ramekins and fold the excess cheesecloth over the top. Refrigerate overnight.

Place the sugar, water and cinnamon stick in a small pot and bring to a boil. Reduce the heat to medium and simmer for 15 minutes. While the sugar syrup is cooking, wash the strawberries and remove the hulls. Cut the larger strawberries in quarters and the smaller ones in half. Add to the sugar syrup and poach for 5 minutes. Remove from the heat and cool. (The poached strawberries may be made up to 1 day ahead. Cover and refrigerate.)

To serve, carefully tug on the cheesecloth to remove the mousse from the ramekins. They will be soft, so handle them carefully. Holding the ramekin in one hand, open the top of the cheesecloth. Place an individual serving plate over the ramekin and invert the mousse onto the plate. Carefully remove the cheesecloth. Repeat with each mousse. Pour the berries and syrup around them, garnish with basil sprigs and serve.

Easy Crème Anglaise

This crème anglaise requires no stirring of the pot and is almost foolproof.

Makes 4 cups (1L)

4 cups	half-and-half cream	1 L
1/4 cup	granulated sugar	60 ml
8	large egg yolks	8

Place the cream and sugar in a large saucepan and bring to a full rolling boil. While waiting for the cream to boil, whisk the egg yolks together.

As soon as the cream reaches a frothy boil, remove from the heat and whisk in a thin stream into the egg yolks. Strain through a sieve and refrigerate, whisking occasionally until cold. (Keeps for 3 days, covered and refrigerated.)

Lavender Crème Anglaise with Fresh Berries

I was about 20 when I first encountered lavender in food. I viewed my friend Judy, 5 or 6 years older than me, as a food-savvy sophisticate.

To make a salad dressing, she put a few pinches of herbes de provence in a mortar and pounded it with a clove of garlic and some salt. She added rice vinegar and French olive oil, then tossed it with the salad. The sweet flavor of the lavender haunted me for days afterwards.

Serves 6-8

4 cups	half-and-half cream	1 L
1/4 cup	granulated sugar	60 ml
1 Tbsp.	fresh lavender leaves, loosely packed	15 ml
8	large egg yolks	8
1/2 pt.	fresh raspberries, picked over	250 ml
1/2 pt.	fresh blueberries, picked over	250 ml
1/2 pt.	fresh strawberries, picked over	250 ml
1/2 pt.	fresh blackberries, picked over	250 ml

To make the crème anglaise, place the cream, sugar and lavender in a large saucepan and bring to a full rolling boil.

While waiting for the cream to boil, whisk the egg yolks together.

As soon as the cream reaches a frothy boil, remove from the heat and whisk it in a thin stream into the egg yolks. Strain through a sieve and refrigerate, whisking occasionally until cold. (Keeps for 3 days, covered and refrigerated.)

When you are ready to serve the dessert, quickly wash and drain the berries if necessary. Cut the strawberries in halves and quarters if they are large. You can arrange rows of berries on a platter, scatter them in an abstract manner or, more formally, layer them in martini or balloon wine glasses. Serve the pitcher of crème anglaise on the side.

Basil Crème Anglaise

Serve this with fresh sliced peaches or strawberries, as well as the pears poached in gerwurztraminer.

Makes 4 cups (1 L)

4 cups	half-and-half cream	1 L
1/4 cup	granulated sugar	60 ml
1	3-inch (7.5-cm) cinnamon stick	1
1/2	of a whole nutmeg, coarsely chopped	1/2
8	large egg yolks	8
1/2 cup	loosely packed basil leaves	125 ml

Place the cream, sugar, cinnamon stick and nutmeg in a large saucepan and bring to a full rolling boil.

While waiting for the mixture to boil, whisk the egg yolks together.

As soon as the cream reaches a frothy boil, remove from the heat and whisk it in a thin stream into the egg yolks. Strain through a sieve and refrigerate, whisking occasionally until cold. (The crème anglaise may be prepared up to 2 days in advance, covered and refrigerated.)

Bring a small pot of water to a boil. Add the basil leaves and stir a few times, then strain immediately through a sieve and cool under cold water. Drain and squeeze gently to remove the water.

Purée the basil and 1 cup (250 ml) of the crème anglaise in a food processor or blender. Stir the mixture into the remaining cold crème anglaise. Keep refrigerated and serve within 8 hours of making.

Pears Poached in Riesling with Basil Crème Anglaise

White-wine poached pears with a splash of raspberry or strawberry purée make a good dessert, but the Basil Crème Anglaise adds a touch of elegance.

Serves 6

2 cups	Riesling wine	500 ml
1 1/2 cups	sugar	375 ml
1	3-inch (7.5-cm) stick cinnamon	1
1/2 tsp.	whole coriander seeds	2.5 ml
	peel of one lemon	
6	well-shaped, slightly under-ripe pears with long stems	6
1 recipe	Basil Crème Anglaise, opposite	1 recipe

Combine the wine, sugar, cinnamon stick, coriander seeds and lemon peel in a large noncorrodible pot that can accommodate the pears lying down. Bring to a simmer.

Carefully peel the pears, leaving the stems intact. Using a melon baller, carefully cut the cores out from the bottom. As each pear is done, drop it into the wine syrup.

When all the pears are done, add enough water to the wine syrup to make the pears float. Bring to a gentle simmer and poach gently until the pears are completely tender, about 30 minutes to 1 hour, depending on the ripeness of the pears. When they are done, transfer them carefully with a slotted spoon, stem side up, to a shallow dish. Strain the wine syrup and discard the seasonings.

Place the syrup back in the pot and bring to a boil. Continue boiling until the syrup has greatly reduced and becomes thick and sticky. Pour over the pears and cool completely. Serve in a pool of Basil Crème Anglaise.

Pears Poached with Red Wine, Rosemary and Black Pepper

There is much to admire in a red wine poached pear: its soft, rounded shape with an elegant stem, the firm but soft texture to the bite, and its hypnotic red glaze.

Serves 6

2 cups	dry red wine	500 ml
1 1/2 cups	sugar	375 ml
1	3-inch (7.5-cm) stick cinnamon	1
3	whole cloves	3
16	whole black peppercorns	16
2	sprigs fresh rosemary	2
6	well-shaped, slightly under-ripe pears with long stems	6

Combine the red wine, sugar, cinnamon, cloves, peppercorns and rosemary in a large noncorrodible pot that can accommodate the pears lying down. Bring to a simmer.

Carefully peel the pears, leaving the stems intact. Using a melon baller, carefully cut the cores out from the bottom. As each pear is done, place it into the red wine syrup.

When all the pears are done, add enough water to the red wine syrup to make the pears float. Bring to a gentle simmer and poach gently until the pears are completely tender, about 30 minutes to 1 hour, depending on the ripeness of the pears. When they are done, transfer them carefully with a slotted spoon, stem side up, to a shallow dish. Strain the red wine syrup and discard the seasonings.

Place the syrup back in the pot and bring to a boil. Continue boiling until the syrup has greatly reduced and becomes thick and sticky. Pour over the pears.

Baste the pears with syrup whenever you remember to. The more basting, the more glazed and better-looking the pears will be. Serve at room temperature with lightly whipped cream or Crème Fraîche (page 192) cascading down the side or in a pool of Crème Anglaise (page 163).

Grilled Peaches with Raspberry Purée

An updated Peach Melba, easy to make on the barbecue after you have finished grilling dinner. Serve with Crème Fraîche (page 192), or, if you want to go all out, a spill of fresh blueberries or strawberries.

Serves 6

2 pts.	fresh raspberries	1 L
1/2 cup	sugar	125 ml
6	ripe, juicy peaches	6
2 Tbsp.	brown sugar	30 ml
4 Tbsp.	rum or brandy	60 ml

To make the raspberry purée, process the raspberries and sugar until smooth in the work bowl of a food processor or blender. Press the purée through a sieve with the back of a spoon to remove the seeds. To make this by hand, place the raspberries and sugar in a large bowl and mash with a potato masher until completely mushed. Sieve as above.

Simmer the peaches in a large pot of boiling water for 20 seconds. Put the peaches in cold water to stop the cooking and remove the skins. Cut each peach in half and remove the pit.

Mix the brown sugar and rum or brandy together.

Preheat the barbecue. Grill the peaches cut side down until they are lightly marked and slightly translucent, about 3-5 minutes. Turn them over. Carefully place a spoonful of the brown sugar mixture in each hollow. Continue grilling for 3-5 minutes more. Carefully transfer the peach halves to plates. Drizzle the raspberry purée over them and serve immediately.

Rhubarb Compote

Serve warm, sprinkled with cinnamon, and buttered toast on the side, for an instant comfort food.

Makes about 4 cups (1 L)

2 lbs.	fresh young rhubarb with pink stems	900 g
1 1/2 cups	sugar	375 ml
1/4 cup	water	60 ml

Trim the leaves and the lower end of the stalks from the rhubarb and cut into 1-inch (2.5-cm) chunks. Place in a noncorrodible saucepan with the sugar and water. Cover and set over low heat. Stew gently for at least an hour. The slower it cooks the better, as the rhubarb retains its shape. Remove from the heat and cool in a bowl. Cover and refrigerate. The compote will keep for 2 weeks.

Ginger and Poppy Seed Parfait with Rhubarb Compote

A great make-ahead dessert and a fine way to celebrate fresh spring rhubarb.

Serves 6

3/4 lb.	fresh ginger	350 g
1 1/4 cups	whipping cream	310 ml
1/4 cup	milk	60 ml
6	egg yolks	6
1 Tbsp.	white sugar	15 ml
1/4 lb.	white chocolate	115 g
2 tsp.	molasses	10 ml
2 Tbsp.	sour cream	30 ml
2 Tbsp.	toasted poppy seeds	30 ml
1 recipe	Rhubarb Compote, page 167	1 recipe

Slice the ginger into 1/4-inch-thick (.5-cm) slices. You should have about 1 1/2 cups (375 ml). Place the ginger in a saucepan and cover with water. Bring to a boil and boil for 30 seconds. Drain well.

Scald 3/4 cup (185 ml) of the cream with the milk and the blanched ginger. Remove from the heat. Cover and let stand for 30 minutes. Strain and discard the ginger. Return the cream to the saucepan and reheat.

While it is reheating, beat the egg yolks and sugar together until the sugar has dissolved and the mixture is thick and pale yellow. Pour 1/4 of the hot cream mixture into the egg yolks, beating continuously. Return the mixture to the remaining cream in the saucepan. Cook over medium-high heat, whisking constantly, until the mixture just reaches the boiling point. Immediately remove from the heat and add the white chocolate, stirring until it melts. Strain into the bowl of an electric mixer. Add the molasses. Beat at low speed for 10 minutes until thick and mousselike and the underside of the bowl is cold. Refrigerate until cold, about 30 minutes.

Beat the remaining 1/2 cup (125 ml) cream and sour cream until it forms soft peaks. Fold into the cold ginger mixture along with the poppy seeds. Pour into an 8-inch (10-cm) ring mold, loaf pan or mold of your choice and freeze until firm, about 4 hours. Unmold by dipping in a pan of hot water. Cut into slices and serve with the rhubarb compote.

Baked Apples with Red Wine and Cinnamon

An adult version of apples baked with cinnamon hearts, but not necessarily better.

Serves 6

4	large apples	4
6 Tbsp.	unsalted butter	90 ml
3 Tbsp.	brown sugar	45 ml
1 Tbsp.	flour	15 ml
1 cup	water	250 ml
2 1/2 cups	red wine	625 ml
3/4 cup	sugar	185 ml
1	cinnamon stick, broken into 1-inch (2.5-cm) pieces	1
2	whole cloves	2
6	whole black peppercorns	6
4	large sprigs thyme	4

Preheat the oven to 350°F (180°C). Core the apples and peel a 1-inch (2.5-cm) strip of peel from the middle of each apple. Mix the butter, brown sugar and flour together with your fingertips until crumbly. Lightly butter a baking dish that will fit the apples snugly. Place the apples in the dish and fill each with the brown sugar mixture. Pour 1/2 cup (125 ml) of the water around the apples. Cover with a lid or tin foil and bake for 1 1/2 hours, basting every 15 minutes until the apples are tender.

Place the red wine, sugar, cinnamon, cloves, peppercorns, thyme and the remaining water in a noncorrodible saucepan. Bring to a boil and simmer until the wine is syrupy and reduced by half. Remove the spices. Pour the spiced wine over the apples, cover, and bake for 15 minutes longer. Remove from the oven and serve warm with lightly whipped cream, if desired.

Apple Crepes with Apple Cider Sauce

This is a bit time-consuming, but the crepes and filling can be prepared 2 or 3 days in advance, covered and refrigerated. The only thing left to do right before serving is making the sauce.

Makes 16 crepes, serving 6-8

Crepes

1 cup	all-purpose flour	250 ml
1 1/3 cups	milk	330 ml
1/4 cup	water	60 ml
1/4 cup	nonalcoholic still apple cider	60 ml
3	large eggs	3
2	egg yolks	2
2 Tbsp.	sugar	30 ml
1/8 tsp.	ground nutmeg	.5 ml
1/2 tsp.	ground cinnamon	2.5 ml

Filling

6	large Granny Smith apples	6
2 Tbsp.	lemon juice	30 ml
1 1/2 cups	granulated sugar	375 ml
1/2 cup	water	125 ml
2 Tbsp.	unsalted butter	30 ml

Cider Sauce

1 cup	nonalcoholic still apple cider	250 ml
1/4 cup	apple cider vinegar	60 ml
1 tsp.	vanilla extract	5 ml
	pinch of cinnamon	
2 Tbsp.	granulated sugar	30 ml
6 oz.	cold unsalted butter, cut into 1/2-inch (1-cm) cubes	180 ml

To make the crepe batter, place the flour in a bowl. Beat the remaining batter ingredients together and beat into the flour until smooth. Cover with plastic wrap. Let stand at room temperature for 1 hour or refrigerate overnight.

To prepare the filling, preheat the oven to 350°F (180°C). Peel, core and slice the apples into 1/4-inch (.5-cm) slices. Toss with the lemon juice and set aside. In a small, heavy saucepan, bring the sugar and water to a boil over medium heat and cook until it becomes caramel-colored. Pour into an ovenproof baking dish large enough to hold the apples and rotate it so the bottom is covered with caramel.

Pour the apples over the caramel and dot with the butter. Cover the dish with foil and bake for 15 minutes. Remove from the oven and stir well. Cover and bake for 15 minutes longer. The apples should be smooth and spreadable. If not, bake covered for 10-15 minutes longer. Remove and let cool. (The filling may be made 2 days in advance. Cover and refrigerate.)

To make the crepes, heat a 6- to 7-inch (15- to 18-cm) crepe or omelette pan over medium heat. Brush the pan with oil. Add 2-3 Tbsp. (30-45 ml) of the crepe batter and rotate to cover the bottom of the pan. Cook for 1-2 minutes until set. Flip over and cook 1 minute longer. Continue with the remaining batter, stacking the crepes on top of each other. (The crepes may be made 2 days in advance. Wrap tightly and refrigerate.)

To assemble the crepes, butter a large shallow pan. Spread one side of each crepe with the apple mixture. Fold into quarters. Continue with the remaining crepes. Place in a single layer in the pan. Cover with tin foil.

Combine the cider, cider vinegar, vanilla and cinnamon in a saucepan. Reduce to 3 Tbsp. (45 ml). Add the sugar and remove from the heat.

Preheat the oven to 400°F (200°C). Bake the crepes for 6-8 minutes, until heated through. While the crepes are heating, rewarm the cider mixture and cut the butter into 1-inch (2.5-cm) cubes. Whisk the butter cubes one at a time into the sauce, never letting it boil. Keep the finished sauce warm over low heat.

Serve the crepes on heated plates or a platter, surrounded with the sauce.

Chocolate and Porter Silk Pie

When I plan dinners for beermakers, the first step is some playful food and beer tasting for potential pairings. I run back and forth from the kitchen to the table, with bits of spices, herbs, cheese, vegetables—whatever!

But when it came to the porter, we were having trouble. Chocolate was suggested. We tasted, sipped, froze. The chocolate and porter combined to create the flavor of chocolate-covered maraschino cherries!

Andrew decided to use porter instead of coffee in my recipe for chocolate silk pie. It worked like a charm.

If you don't want to use the porter, substitute strong black coffee instead.

Makes 1 9-inch (22-cm) pie

1 recipe	Chocolate Pastry	1 recipe
6 Tbsp.	rich, fruity porter	90 ml
1 cup	unsalted butter	250 ml
1/4 cup	granulated sugar	60 ml
9 oz.	bittersweet chocolate, finely chopped	270 g
1/4 tsp.	salt	1.2 ml
6	large egg yolks, at room temperature	6
1 cup	whipping cream	250 ml

Preheat the oven to 350°F (180°C). Press the pastry evenly into a 9-inch (22-cm) pie pan. Chill for 30 minutes. Prick with a fork and weight (see Prebaking a Pie Shell, page 190). Bake for 15 minutes. Remove the weights and cook for 10-15 minutes longer until the pastry is completely dry and cooked through. Cool.

Combine the porter, butter and sugar in a saucepan. Bring to a boil and add the chocolate. Remove from the heat and whisk until the chocolate is completely melted and smooth. Scrape into a bowl. With a whisk or electric mixer, beat in the egg yolks one at a time. Mix in the salt. Cool to room temperature.

Chocolate Pastry

Makes 1 9-inch (22-cm) pie shell

1 cup	all-purpose flour	250 ml
1/2 cup	granulated sugar	125 ml
1/2 cup	cocoa	125 ml
3/4 cup	cold unsalted butter, cut into 1/2-inch (1-cm) cubes	185 ml
1	large egg, beaten	1

Place the flour, sugar and cocoa in the work bowl of a food processor and pulse a few times to combine. Scatter the butter on top and pulse until mealy. Pour the egg through the feed tube and pulse briefly. The dough should not come together in a ball. Turn out the pastry and gently form a loose ball. Cover and set aside at room temperature for 30 minutes before using. If you are not using the pastry immediately, wrap tightly and refrigerate for up to 5 days or freeze for up to one month.

Pour half of the chocolate mixture into the cooled pie shell and refrigerate. Place the other half in the fridge as well. Stir the mixture in the bowl frequently until it is cold but not firm.

Whip the cream to soft peaks and fold into the cooled chocolate. Pile onto the pie in decorative swirls or use a pastry bag if you are feeling ambitious. Chill until set, about 4 hours. Keeps well for 4 days, refrigerated.

Ethereal Chocolate Cream

Lighter than the lightest cheesecake, with crisp flakes of chocolate that melt in your mouth, and profoundly simple in ingredients and execution, this is one of the most delicious summer desserts you can make.

It is important that the crème fraîche be very cold and the chocolate hot. You want to achieve wisps of chocolate that have a crunch when the dessert is cold.

Serves 4-6

2 cups	Crème Fraîche, page 192, well chilled	500 ml
6 Tbsp.	icing sugar	90 ml
4 oz.	hot, melted, bittersweet chocolate	115 g
	fresh berries of your choice	

Whip the crème fraîche and icing sugar with a whisk until the mixture mounds lightly. Fold in the chocolate to form long streaks in the crème fraîche.

Line a 2-cup (500-ml) *couer à la crème* mold or a small, shallow, clean basket (it will leave a lovely basket-weave imprint on the cream) with a piece of cheesecloth large enough to enclose the top. (Couer à la crème molds are ceramic, heart-shaped molds with drainage holes in the bottom. Most good kitchenware stores carry them.) Pour in the crème fraîche mixture and smooth the top. Bring the overhanging cheesecloth over the top. Cover with plastic wrap, place on a plate to catch the drips and refrigerate overnight.

To serve, unfold the top of the cheesecloth and center a plate over the mold. Flip the whole arrangement over and slip off the mold. Remove the cheesecloth. Surround with the fresh berries and serve immediately.

Espresso Granita with Vanilla Ice Cream

We of the Pacific Northwest love coffee. In fact, this geographic area is sometimes called latte land, a twist on a more common appellation—la la land. This makes a lovely, simple dessert—refreshing and creamy at the same time.

Serves 4-6

1 cup	espresso or extremely strong coffee made from an espresso roast	250 ml
1/2 cup	sugar	125 ml
3/4 cup	cold water	185 ml
	vanilla ice cream	

To make the granita, combine the hot espresso with the sugar and stir until dissolved. Add the cold water and pour the mixture into a shallow pan that will fit in the freezer. Stir every 15 minutes with a whisk, breaking up the clumps of ice crystals until frozen.

To serve, place a scoop of vanilla ice cream in an individual dish, wine glass or martini glass. Place a scoop of granita on top. (The granita will not scoop neatly like ice cream; this is how it should be.) Garnish with a few coffee beans and serve immediately.

PACIFIC PASSIONS
A Bit
of
Baking

Trevor's Apricot, Ginger and Black Pepper Biscotti

My colleague Trevor developed this recipe for a dessert wine competition. All of the kitchen got involved in the process, making suggestions and tasting. Alas, his recipe did not win, but it was a winner as far as we were concerned.

Makes about 30 biscotti

3 cups	all-purpose flour	750 ml
1 cup	granulated sugar	250 ml
1 tsp.	salt	5 ml
1 1/2 tsp.	coarsely ground black pepper	7.5 ml
2 1/2 tsp.	baking powder	12.5 ml
1 Tbsp.	fresh ginger, grated	15 ml
3/4 cup	unsalted butter, chilled and cut into 1/2-inch (1-cm) cubes	185 ml
1 cup	whole almonds, roasted	250 ml
2	eggs	2
2 Tbsp.	sweet dessert wine	30 ml
3/4 cup	dried apricots, julienned	185 ml

Place the flour, sugar, salt, pepper, baking powder and ginger in the work bowl of a food processor. Pulse a few times to combine the ingredients.

Scatter the butter over the top of the flour mixture and pulse until a fine meal forms. Add the almonds and pulse a few more times to chop them coarsely.

Beat the eggs and wine together. Add the apricots and the flour-butter mixture. Mix only until combined.

Preheat the oven to 350°F (180°C). Line a baking sheet with parchment paper. Divide the dough in two and shape into logs that are 3 inches (7.5 cm) across. Refrigerate for 1/2 hour.

Bake for 20-30 minutes until golden brown. Remove from the oven and cool completely. Slice on a deep diagonal into 1 1/2-inch (4-cm) slices. Place on the baking sheet without the slices touching and bake for 10 minutes longer. Remove and cool on wire racks. Store in an airtight tin.

Batter Bread

Batter bread is a cousin to brioche. It is light and buttery and can carry many seasonings, both sweet and savory. It makes great French toast and is easily made in a mixer.

Makes 1 18-inch (45-cm) loaf

3/4 cup	lukewarm milk	185 ml
1 Tbsp.	granulated sugar	15 ml
1 Tbsp.	dry yeast	15 ml
1 1/4 tsp.	salt	6.2 ml
2	large eggs	2
1/2 cup.	unsalted butter, softened	125 ml
3 cups	all-purpose flour	750 ml
1 Tbsp.	butter	15 ml
1	egg yolk	1
2 Tbsp.	water	30 ml

Stir the milk and sugar together in a large bowl or the work bowl of an electric mixer. Stir in the yeast and let the mixture work for 10 minutes.

Add the 1/2 cup (125 ml) butter, eggs and salt. With the dough hook attachment or by hand, beat in half of the flour. Beat vigorously for 5 minutes. Beat in the remaining flour 1/4 cup (60 ml) at a time. Remove from the bowl and lightly knead into a ball.

Place the ball of dough in a large, lightly oiled bowl. Cover the bowl with a towel or plastic wrap and let rise in a warm place until doubled in bulk, about 1 hour.

Butter a deep 8-inch (20-cm) round cake pan with 1 Tbsp. (15 ml) butter. Punch down the dough and form into a round loaf. Place the dough in the pan, smooth side up. Cover and let rise until doubled, about 30 minutes. Preheat the oven to 375°F (190°C).

Beat the egg yolk and water together and brush the top of the bread thickly with the mixture. Bake the bread for 35 minutes until nicely browned. Unmold onto a cooling rack and let cool completely before slicing.

Soda Bread

This delicious bread requires no kneading or rising time. I like to make tomato or cucumber sandwiches with it at the height of summer. For a variation, try adding 2 cups (500 ml) currants and 2 Tbsp. (30 ml) caraway seeds.

Makes 2 loaves

4 cups	buttermilk	1 L
1/4 cup	honey	60 ml
2 cups	unbleached white flour	500 ml
4 cups	whole wheat flour	1 L
1 Tbsp.	baking soda, sifted	15 ml
1 1/2 tsp.	salt	7.5 ml

Preheat the oven to 350°F (180°C). Mix the buttermilk and honey in a large bowl until well blended. Stir the dry ingredients together. Add the dry ingredients all at once to the wet ingredients and stir only until combined.

Divide the dough into 2 equal portions. Shape each portion into an oval about 10 inches (25 cm) long and 5 inches (12.5 cm) wide. Place the loaves on a large baking sheet lined with parchment paper. Make a slash about 1/4 inch (.5 cm) deep down the middle of each loaf.

Bake for about 50 minutes, or until the loaf sounds hollow when tapped on the bottom. Remove from the pan and cool on a rack.

Black Pepper and Onion Soda Bread

I thought that plain soda bread was great until Carmen came up with this version. It has been met with accolades from customers and staff.

Makes 2 loaves

1 1/2 Tbsp.	whole black peppercorns	20 ml
1	thinly sliced onion	1
1 Tbsp.	vegetable oil	15 ml
1 recipe	Soda Bread, above	1 recipe
1	egg, beaten	1
1 tsp.	coarse salt	5 ml

Dry-roast the peppercorns in a heavy frying pan until fragrant. Cool and crush coarsely.

Sauté the onions in the oil until golden brown. Place in a sieve to drain and set aside to cool.

Follow the recipe for soda bread, adding the onions and cracked black pepper with the flour mixture to the buttermilk and honey. Proceed as in the soda bread recipe for mixing and shaping the loaves. When the loaves are shaped, brush with the beaten egg and sprinkle with the coarse salt. Bake and cool as in the soda bread recipe.

Beer Bread

We have so many good micro-breweries in the Pacific Northwest. This recipe provides a perfect opportunity to capture their unique flavors—and it makes great cheese sandwiches.

Makes 2 loaves

2 Tbsp.	molasses	30 ml
2 cups	beer, heated to lukewarm	500 ml
1 Tbsp.	dry yeast	15 ml
1 1/2 cups	whole wheat flour	375 ml
2 tsp.	salt	10 ml
1/4 cup	olive oil	60 ml
4 1/2-5 cups	all-purpose flour	1.12-1.25 L
	cornmeal	

Combine the molasses and beer in a large mixing bowl and stir well. Stir in the yeast and let stand until the yeast foams, about 10 minutes.

Stir in the whole wheat flour, salt and olive oil. Work in the all-purpose flour, one cup at a time, to make a stiff dough. When you can add no more flour, turn the contents of the bowl out onto the counter and knead for 10 minutes, adding flour as necessary to prevent the dough from sticking.

Lightly oil a large bowl. Place the dough in the bowl and roll it around to coat it with the oil. Cover with plastic wrap and let it rise in a warm place until doubled in bulk, about 1 1/2 hours. Punch down the bread and form into a ball. Let rise again, covered, for 1 hour.

Remove the dough from the bowl and place on a lightly floured surface. Divide into six equal pieces and roll each piece into a rope 12-14 inches (30-35 cm) long. Tightly braid three of the ropes together. Do the same with the remaining ropes. Place the loaves 3 inches (7.5 cm) apart on a baking sheet that has been sprinkled with cornmeal. Cover and let rise in a warm place until doubled, about 45 minutes.

Preheat the oven to 450°F (230°C). Place a pan of boiling water on the lower rack of the oven. Lightly brush or spray the breads with water and place in the oven. Bake for 30-40 minutes until the loaves are brown and crusty and sound hollow when tapped on the bottom. Remove to a rack to cool.

Whole-Wheat and Coriander Wafers

I love the spicy orange scent and flavor of crushed coriander seeds. These wafers are good with hard cheeses, such as Gouda and cheddar, as well as blue cheeses.

Makes 40 or more wafers, depending on how you cut them

3 1/3 cups	whole-wheat flour	830 ml
1/8 tsp.	baking soda	.5 ml
1/2 tsp.	salt	2.5 ml
2 Tbsp.	granulated sugar	30 ml
1/2 cup	unsalted butter at room temperature	125 ml
1 Tbsp.	coarsely crushed coriander seeds	15 ml
1	large egg	1
1 1/4 cups	water	310 ml

Preheat the oven to 325°F (160°C). Sift the flour, baking soda, salt and sugar together. With an electric mixer or by hand, cream the butter. Add the flour mixture and coriander seeds and mix until mealy. Beat the egg and water together. Add to the flour mixture and combine only until the mixture holds together.

Turn the dough out onto a floured surface and knead lightly. Divide the dough in half. Roll out one piece on a floured surface to 1/8 inch (.3 cm) thick. Prick the dough thoroughly with a fork. Cut into 3-inch (7.5-cm) squares, rounds or diamonds and place close together on parchment-lined baking sheets. Continue with the remaining dough, saving and rerolling the scraps into wafers.

Bake for 20-25 minutes, until the wafers are golden brown. Transfer to a rack to cool. Store in an airtight container.

Sweet Oat Cakes

These are sweet enough to be a cookie and a handsome vehicle for butter or cheese.

Makes 35-40 oat cakes

2 cups	all-purpose flour	500 ml
1 1/2 cups	rolled oats	375 ml
1/2 cup	brown sugar	125 ml
1 tsp.	salt	5 ml
1/2 tsp.	baking soda	2.5 ml
3/4 cup	unsalted butter, chilled and cut into 1/2-inch (1-cm) cubes	185 ml
1/2 cup	cold water	125 ml

Preheat the oven to 350°F (180°C). In a large bowl, stir the dry ingredients together. Work in the butter with your fingertips until it is thoroughly blended. Add the water and mix just until the dough holds together.

Divide the dough into four pieces. On a floured surface, roll the dough, one piece at a time, to 1/8-inch (.3-cm) thickness. Cut into 3-inch (7.5-cm) squares and place close together on parchment-lined baking sheets. Save the scraps and reroll them.

Bake for 10-15 minutes, until golden brown. Remove from the pan and cool on wire racks. Store in an airtight container.

Oatmeal and Sesame Crackers

These are not like store-bought crackers. They are hearty, crunchy and chewy. Serve them alongside the sweet oat cakes for a contrast of taste and texture.

There are many good cold-pressed oils on the market. Try one of the nut ones (roasted sesame is a bit overwhelming) to vary the flavor of the crackers.

Makes 30-40 crackers

2 cups	stone-ground whole-wheat flour	500 ml
1 1/2 cups	rolled oats	375 ml
1/2 tsp.	salt	2.5 ml
3 Tbsp.	black sesame seeds, toasted (see page 17)	45 ml
3/4 cup	water	185 ml
1/3 cup	vegetable oil	80 ml
	extra vegetable oil for brushing the tops of the crackers	

Preheat the oven to 350°F (180°C). Stir the flour, oats, salt and sesame seeds together. Whisk the water and oil together until milky. Stir into the dry mixture and knead on a floured surface for 5 minutes.

Divide the dough in half. Roll out the pieces on a floured surface, one at a time, to 1/8 inch (.3 cm) thick. Brush lightly with vegetable oil and cut the dough into 3-inch (7.5-cm) squares or diamonds. Place close together on parchment-lined baking sheets. Reroll the scraps and cut them into more crackers. Bake for 15 minutes, until golden brown. Cool on wire racks. Store in an airtight container.

Cheddar Loonies

These are good with soups and salads or just as snacks.

Makes 36 loonies

1 1/4 cups	all-purpose flour	310 ml
1/8 tsp.	salt	.5 ml
4 Tbsp.	unsalted butter, melted	60 ml
1/2 lb.	aged orange cheddar, grated	225 g

Place the flour and salt in the work bowl of a food processor. Pulse several times to blend. Add the butter and cheese and pulse until the mixture is well blended but still crumbly. Turn onto a floured surface and knead until smooth. Form into a log 1 1/2 inches (4 cm) in diameter. Wrap in plastic wrap and chill for 1 hour. (The dough may be prepared to this point several days in advance. Freeze for longer storage.)

Preheat the oven to 350°F (180°C). Slice the log into 1/4-inch (.5-cm) slices. Place 1/2 inch (1 cm) apart on baking sheets lined with parchment paper. Bake for 10-12 minutes until golden brown.

To vary the loonies, brush them with egg wash (1 egg beaten with 2 tsp./10 ml water) and sprinkle them with different flavorings before baking. Black or white sesame seeds, crushed walnuts, poppy seeds, cumin seeds, caraway seeds and chili flakes are all good choices.

Okanagan Apple Muffins

If you only make one muffin from this book, it should be this one.

Makes 15 muffins

1/2 cup	brown sugar, firmly packed	125 ml
6 Tbsp.	all-purpose flour	90 ml
1/4 cup	unsalted butter, melted	60 ml
1 tsp.	ground cinnamon	5 ml
1 1/2 cups	brown sugar, firmly packed	375 ml
2/3 cup	vegetable oil	160 ml
1	large egg	1
1 tsp.	vanilla	5 ml
1 cup	water	250 ml
2 tsp.	apple cider vinegar	10 ml
2 1/2 cups	all-purpose flour	625 ml
1 tsp.	baking soda	5 ml
1/2 tsp.	salt	2.5 ml
2 cups	peeled apple, diced into 1/2-inch (1-cm) chunks	500 ml

Preheat the oven to 325°F (160°C). Butter and flour a 15-cup muffin tin or line with paper cups if desired.

To make the topping, combine the 1/2 cup (125 ml) brown sugar, 6 Tbsp. (90 ml) flour, butter and cinnamon in a bowl. Mix with your fingers until crumbly. Set aside. Beat the 1 1/2 cups (375 ml) brown sugar, oil, egg and vanilla together in a large bowl. Combine the water and vinegar. Sift the flour, soda and salt together and blend into the oil mixture alternately with the water. Add the diced apple and mix until just combined. Spoon into the prepared muffin pan and sprinkle generously with the topping.

Bake for 30 minutes, until golden brown and the top springs back when lightly touched.

Blueberry Muffins with Hazelnut Streusel

The streusel adds a sweet crunch to the taste.

Makes 8 muffins

1/4 cup	sugar	60 ml
1/4 cup	finely ground hazelnuts	60 ml
1/2 tsp.	cinnamon	2.5 ml
1 Tbsp.	unsalted butter, melted	15 ml
1/4 cup	unsalted butter	60 ml
1/2 cup	sugar	125 ml
1	large egg	1
3/4 tsp.	vanilla	4 ml
1 cup	all-purpose flour	250 ml
1 tsp.	baking powder	5 ml
1/4 tsp.	salt	1.2 ml
1/3 cup	milk	80 ml
1 1/2 cups	blueberries, fresh or frozen	375 ml

To make the streusel, combine the 1/4 cup (60 ml) sugar, hazelnuts and cinnamon in a small bowl. Add the 1 Tbsp. (15 ml) melted butter and mix until crumbly. Set aside.

Preheat the oven to 375°F (190°C). Butter and flour an 8-cup muffin tin, or line with paper cups if you wish.

In a large bowl, cream the 1/4 cup (60 ml) butter and 1/2 cup (125 ml) sugar together until light and fluffy. Beat in the egg and vanilla. Sift the dry ingredients together and add to the creamed mixture along with the milk. Stir with a fork until just combined (a few lumps are okay). Gently fold in the blueberries. Spoon into the prepared muffin tin and top with the streusel.

Bake for 25-30 minutes, until golden brown and the top springs back when lightly touched.

Rhubarb and Raspberry Muffins

Always a popular muffin in this part of the world.

Makes 12 muffins

1	large egg	1
1 cup	brown sugar	250 ml
1/4 cup	unsalted butter, melted	60 ml
3/4 cup	sour cream or yogurt	185 ml
2 cups	all-purpose flour	500 ml
1 tsp.	baking soda	5 ml
1/4 tsp.	salt	1.2 ml
1/4 tsp.	cinnamon	1.2 ml
3/4 cup	diced rhubarb, fresh or frozen	185 ml
3/4 cup	raspberries, fresh or frozen	185 ml

Preheat the oven to 350°F (180°C). Butter and flour a 12-cup muffin tin or line with paper cups if desired.

Beat the egg, brown sugar, melted butter and sour cream or yogurt together. Sift the flour, baking soda, salt and cinnamon together. Combine the wet and dry ingredients, mixing only until combined. Fold in the rhubarb and raspberries. Spoon into the prepared tin.

Bake for 25-30 minutes, until slightly browned and the top springs back when lightly touched.

Buttermilk and Currant Scones

To vary this recipe, you can substitute 1 cup (250 ml) fresh blueberries for the currants. Or, for cheddar scones, decrease the sugar to 2 Tbsp. (30 ml), omit the currants and add 1 1/4 cups (310 ml) grated aged cheddar to the flour mixture before adding the buttermilk.

Makes 12 scones

3 cups	all-purpose flour	750 ml
1/3 cup	sugar	80 ml
2 1/2 tsp.	baking powder	12.5 ml
1/2 tsp.	baking soda	2.5 ml
3/4 cup	unsalted butter, chilled	185 ml
3/4 cup	dried currants	185 ml
1 cup	buttermilk	250 ml
2 Tbsp.	whipping cream	30 ml

Preheat the oven to 375°F (190°C). Lightly butter a baking sheet. Sift the dry ingredients together in a large bowl. Cut the butter into 1/2-inch (1-cm) cubes and toss with the flour mixture. With a pastry blender or 2 knives, cut the butter into the dry ingredients until it resembles coarse meal. Toss in the currants. Quickly stir in the buttermilk, mixing only until the mixture holds together.

Turn out onto a lightly floured surface and pat into a large circle, about 1/2 inch (1 cm) thick. Cut into 12 wedges and place 1 inch (2.5 cm) apart on the prepared baking sheet. Brush the tops lightly with the whipping cream. Bake for 10-12 minutes, until golden brown. Transfer to a rack to cool.

Cranberry Scones

Have these scones on Christmas morning with lots of butter and orange marmalade.

Makes 4 large scones

1 3/4 cups	all-purpose flour	435 ml
1/2 cup	cake flour	125 ml
1/2 cup	sugar	125 ml
2 tsp.	baking powder	10 ml
1/4 tsp.	salt	1.2 ml
1/2 tsp.	cinnamon	2.5 ml
1/4 cup	unsalted butter, chilled	60 ml
1 cup	whipping cream	250 ml
3/4 cup	fresh cranberries, or frozen ones that have been thawed	185 ml

Preheat the oven to 375°F (190°C). Lightly butter a baking sheet. Sift the dry ingredients together in a large bowl. Cut the butter into 1/2-inch (1-cm) cubes and toss with the flour mixture.

With a pastry blender or 2 knives, cut the butter into the dry ingredients until the mixture resembles coarse meal. Set aside 2 Tbsp. (30 ml) of the cream. Add the remaining cream and cranberries to the flour mixture and stir only until combined.

Turn the dough out onto a lightly floured surface and pat into a 7-inch (18-cm) circle. Cut into 4 wedges and place well apart on the prepared baking sheet.

Brush lightly with the reserved cream and bake for 15-20 minutes, until golden brown. Place on a rack to cool.

Blueberry Lemon Loaf

Try sandwiching slices of this loaf with strawberry ice cream for a deluxe ice cream sandwich.

Makes 2 small loaves

2 cups	all-purpose flour	500 ml
2 tsp.	baking powder	10 ml
1/2 tsp.	salt	2.5 ml
1/2 cup	unsalted butter, softened	125 ml
1 cup	sugar	250 ml
2	large eggs	2
2 tsp.	vanilla	10 ml
2 Tbsp.	finely grated lemon zest	30 ml
2/3 cup	milk	160 ml
1 1/2 cups	blueberries, fresh or frozen	375 ml

Preheat the oven to 350°F (180°C). Butter and flour two 6- by 3-inch (15- by 7.5-cm) loaf pans.

Sift the flour, baking powder and salt together. Cream the butter and sugar until light and fluffy. Add the eggs one at a time, beating well after each addition. Beat in the vanilla and lemon zest. Add half the flour mixture, beating well, then half the milk. Add the rest of the flour, then the rest of the milk. Gently fold half the blueberries into the batter.

Spoon the batter into the prepared pans. Sprinkle the rest of the berries over the tops of the loaves. Bake for 45-50 minutes, until golden brown and a toothpick inserted into the middle of the loaves comes out clean. Cool in the pans for 10 minutes, then remove to a rack to finish cooling.

Triple Chunk Chocolate Cookies

The chocolate chunk cookie with three different chocolates—therefore, three times as good.

I like to cut chocolate chunks from a good-quality block of chocolate for these cookies. Use a sharp heavy knife to chop the chocolate roughly into 1/4- to 1/2-inch (.6- to 1-cm) chunks.

Makes 30 cookies

2 1/2 cups	all-purpose flour	625 ml
1 tsp.	baking soda	5 ml
1/8 tsp.	salt	.5 ml
1 cup	unsalted butter, at room temperature	250 ml
3/4 cup	granulated sugar	185 ml
1 cup	brown sugar, packed	250 ml
2	large eggs	2
2 tsp.	vanilla	10 ml
1 cup	bittersweet chocolate chunks	250 ml
1 cup	white chocolate chunks	250 ml
1 cup	milk chocolate chunks	250 ml
1 cup	coarsely chopped hazelnuts	250 ml

Preheat oven to 300°F (150°C). Line several baking sheets with parchment paper.

Sift together the flour, baking soda and salt.

Either by hand or with an electric mixer, cream the butter until light. Beat in the sugars until fluffy. Add the eggs one at a time, beating well after each addition. Mix in the vanilla.

Incorporate the flour mixture all at once and mix thoroughly by hand. Stir in the chocolate pieces and nuts. Chill the dough until firm. (The dough may be refrigerated for three days at this point or frozen for up to a month.)

Roll the dough into balls, using about 3 Tbsp. (45 ml) per ball. Place 3 inches (7.5 cm) apart on the parchment-lined baking sheets and flatten with the palm of your hand. Bake for 10 minutes, reverse the baking sheet, and bake for 10 minutes more, or until golden brown around the edges. The cookies should remain slightly soft in the middle. Transfer to cooling racks.

Freezing Cookie Dough

You can form the chilled dough into balls and freeze them in an airtight container. When you want to bake the cookies, remove as many balls as you need and place them on a parchment-lined baking sheet until thawed. Bake according to the recipe.

Sweet Shortcrust Pastry

For this recipe, you need a tart pan with a removable bottom.

Makes 1 9-inch (22-cm) shell

1 1/2 cups	all-purpose flour	375 ml
1/4 cup	granulated sugar	60 ml
3/4 cup	unsalted butter, well chilled	185 ml
1 1/2 tsp.	white vinegar	7.5 ml

Combine the flour and sugar in the work bowl of a food processor fitted with the steel blade. Pulse 2 or 3 times.

Roll the butter in flour (this makes it easier to handle) then cut into 1/2-inch (1-cm) cubes. Distribute them over the flour in the work bowl and process briefly, until the mixture resembles fine meal. Be careful not to process too much.

With the machine running, pour the vinegar through the feed tube and process for 5 seconds. Do not over-process: the dough should still resemble very fine meal and should not gather into a ball.

Remove the dough from the food processor, cover and allow to rest at room temperature for 30 minutes before using.

Gather up a small amount of pastry and knead it between your fingers until it forms a ball. Press this piece into the tart tin. Continue until the bottom and sides of the tin are completely covered. Try to make the pastry as even as possible. Refrigerate the pastry-lined tin for 30 minutes.

Preheat the oven to 375°F (190°C). Place the chilled tart shell in the preheated oven and bake for 20-30 minutes, until pale golden brown and completely cooked. Remove from the oven and allow to cool. When cool, gently remove the pastry shell from the tin.

Savory Pastry

Makes 1 9- to 10-inch (22- to 25-cm) pie or tart

2 cups	all-purpose flour	500 ml
1/2 tsp.	salt	2.5 ml
3/4 cup	unsalted butter, chilled	185 ml
1/3 cup	ice-cold water	80 ml

Combine the flour and salt in a large bowl. Cut the butter into 1/2-inch (1-cm) cubes and place on a plate. Put in the freezer for 5 minutes.

Remove the butter from the freezer and toss with the flour. Add the cold water and knead gently with your fingertips until the mixture forms a shaggy ball. The dough may be used immediately or refrigerated for up to 3 days.

Prebaking a Pie Shell

Preheat the oven to 400°F (200°C). Roll the pastry out to 1/4-inch (.5-cm) thickness and 3 inches (7.5 cm) larger than your pie or tart pan. Roll the pastry around the rolling pin and unroll it over the pie or tart pan. Fit it gently into the corners of the pan and trim the edge flush with the pan if you are using a tart pan. If you are using a pie pan, turn the edge under and crimp.

Prick the bottom of the shell lightly with a fork and line the pan with a piece of tin foil large enough to protrude over the edge. Fill halfway with dried beans or rice.

Bake on the middle shelf of the oven for 15 minutes. Remove the foil and dried beans or rice, return to the oven and bake for 5-10 minutes longer until pale gold.

PACIFIC PASSIONS
The Pacific
Northwest
Pantry

Crème Fraîche

Crème fraîche is cultured cream, similar in flavor to sour cream, with all the properties of whipping cream. Sour cream provides the bacterial culture required. Check the container to make sure that the sour cream you are using does contain bacterial culture.

Makes 2 cups (500 ml)

1/2 cup	sour cream	125 ml
1 1/2 cups	whipping cream	375 ml

Place the sour cream in a bowl and whisk briefly to loosen it up. Slowly whisk in the whipping cream. Don't whip the cream, just make sure it is thoroughly blended. Cover and keep in a warm place overnight. Transfer to a storage container and refrigerate overnight before using. Crème fraîche will keep for 3-4 weeks refrigerated and gets better with age.

Crème fraîche can be heated or reduced without breaking up (as sour cream does) or whipped like whipping cream. It seems to thicken more quickly than whipping cream, so I prefer to use a whisk rather than an electric mixer; it gives me more control over the result.

Blackberry or Marionberry Vinegar

Easy to make and a beautiful color.

Makes 4 cups (1 L)

2 pts.	ripe blackberries or marionberries	1 L
3 cups	white wine vinegar	750 ml
6 Tbsp.	granulated sugar	90 ml

Sort through the berries. Rinse and drain them. Place the berries in a sterilized 2-quart (2-L) jar and crush them with a potato masher or spoon. Add the vinegar and cover the jar tightly. Let stand for 2-4 weeks, shaking the jar occasionally.

Line a sieve with a double layer of dampened cheesecloth and set over a bowl. Strain the vinegar through the cheesecloth. When all the liquid has drained, press the pulp lightly with a spoon. Discard the pulp.

Pour the vinegar into a noncorrodible saucepan and add the sugar. Heat to a simmer, stirring occasionally, until the sugar dissolves. Cool completely.

Place a coffee filter in a funnel and pour the vinegar into a sterilized bottle. (A clear wine bottle is good for this.) Cover with a cap or a clean cork.

Cold Poached Fruit in Red Wine

This is a dual-purpose compote. It goes well alongside pork, ham or roast chicken, or it can accompany a simple cake, gingerbread or, slightly warmed, vanilla ice cream.

Makes about 2 1/2 cups (625 ml)

1 cup	red wine	250 ml
1 cup	water	250 ml
1/2 cup	sugar	125 ml
1	2-inch (5-cm) piece cinnamon stick	1
4	whole cloves	4
10	coriander seeds	10
1	bay leaf	1
10	whole black peppercorns	10
1/2 cup	dried sour cherries or cranberries, loosely packed	125 ml
1/2 cup	dried pears, cut into quarters, loosely packed	125 ml
10	dried figs, cut into quarters	10
1/2 cup	dried apricots, loosely packed	125 ml

At least 2 days in advance, combine all of the ingredients except the dried fruit in a noncorrodible saucepan. Boil for 5 minutes. Place the fruit in a sterilized jar with a 2-inch (5-cm) head space and pour the boiling liquid over the fruit. Cool completely and refrigerate. Keeps indefinitely when refrigerated.

Pickled Ginger

Pickled ginger does require a bit of effort to make, but is far less expensive to make than to buy. Besides, you will have something in your fridge to be proud of. Use it to make the Ginger and Black Bean Vinaigrette, page 83.

Makes about 2 cups (500 ml)

3/4 lb.	ginger, peeled	350 g
2 cups	cider vinegar	500 ml
3/4 cup	sugar	185 ml
4 Tbsp.	salt	60 ml

Using a vegetable peeler, slice the ginger into paper-thin slices with the grain. Cover with boiling water and let stand 2 minutes. Drain well.

Combine the vinegar, sugar and salt in a saucepan. Heat until the sugar is dissolved. Place the ginger in a container with a lid and pour the hot vinegar over it. Stir well, cool, cover and refrigerate. The ginger keeps indefinitely. You may notice a white sediment in the bottom of the container; this is harmless and no cause for concern.

Tomato and Ginger Jam

Not exactly the kind of jam you would spread on toast (although it would be good for the more adventurous), but an excellent condiment for pork, chicken or cheese.

Makes 2 cups (500 ml)

2 1/2 lbs.	ripe plum tomatoes	1 kg
3 Tbsp.	lemon juice	45 ml
1 Tbsp.	finely chopped crystallized ginger	15 ml
2	whole dried chilies	2
1/2 tsp.	salt	2.5 ml
2 1/2 cups	granulated sugar	625 ml
1 1/2 tsp.	ground coriander seeds	7.5 ml
1 tsp.	cumin seeds	5 ml

Bring a large pot of water to a boil. Cut a small X on the bottom of each tomato. Dip the tomatoes, a few at a time, into the water for about 10 seconds. Skin and cut out the stem ends. Cut the tomatoes in half crosswise and squeeze out the seeds and juice into a bowl. Chop the tomatoes into 1/2-inch (1-cm) pieces. Place in a large, noncorrodible saucepan. Place a fine sieve over the pot and strain the lemon juice and the juice from the tomato seeds into the tomatoes. Add the ginger, chilies and salt.

Bring the tomato mixture to a boil, then turn down to a simmer. Cook, stirring occasionally, until the tomatoes are soft, about 15 minutes. Add the sugar. Cook over medium-high heat, stirring constantly.

Place several small saucers in the fridge before you start the jam. To check if the jam is done, place a small amount on a saucer and return it to the fridge until cool (take the jam off the heat when you do this).

When the jam does not run when the saucer is tilted, it is cooked enough. (An easier way is to use an instant-read thermometer; the jam is done when the temperature reaches 220°F/105°C.) When the jam is cooked, remove from the heat and stir in the ground coriander and cumin seeds. Pour into a sterilized jar and cool. The jam keeps indefinitely in the refrigerator.

Sour and Sweet Cherry Ketchup

Fantastic with sausages, roast chicken and pork. You can substitute 3 lbs. (1.3 kg) of marionberries or blackberries for the cherries if you wish. We served this variation with rack of lamb to rave reviews.

Makes 3 cups (750 ml)

1 1/2 lbs.	sour cherries, pitted	675 g
1 1/2 lbs.	sweet cherries, pitted	675 g
3/4 cup	diced onions	185 ml
2 cups	water	500 ml
1/2 cup	dark brown sugar, packed	125 ml
1/2 cup	light corn syrup	125 ml
1/2 cup	cider vinegar	125 ml
3/4 tsp.	ground cinnamon	4 ml
1 tsp.	salt	5 ml
3/4 tsp.	ground ginger	4 ml
1/4 tsp.	ground allspice	1.2 ml
1/4 tsp.	ground cloves	1.2 ml
1/4 tsp.	ground black pepper	1.2 ml

Place the cherries, onions and water in a large saucepan and bring to a boil. Turn the heat down to a simmer and cook for 10 minutes, until the onions are translucent.

Remove from the heat and purée in a food processor or blender until smooth. Return to the saucepan and add the remaining ingredients. Bring to a boil and cook, stirring frequently, until thick, 30-45 minutes.

Place several small saucers in the refrigerator before you start the ketchup. To check for doneness, place a small amount of ketchup on a saucer and return it to the fridge until chilled. Draw your finger through the ketchup. If the track remains, the ketchup is done. Remove the pot from the heat when testing the ketchup to prevent overcooking.

Strain the ketchup through a sieve into a bowl. Cool and transfer to a sterilized jar. Covered and refrigerated, it keeps indefinitely.

Puréeing

When you have to purée food that has a large amount of water in it, such as a soup, strain out the solids with a sieve and reserve the liquid. Purée in a food processor or blender, using some of the reserved liquid to help it along. Return the remaining liquid to the solids when the puréeing is finished.

Stove-Top Roasted Garlic

This is much easier than the traditional way of roasting whole bulbs in the oven, and it gives you greater control over the finished product. Use the cloves and the oil in sauces, mashed potatoes and vinaigrettes or as a garnish for meat, fish or vegetables.

Makes 1 1/2 pint (250 ml) jar

4	heads garlic	4
	vegetable or olive oil	

For stove-top roasted garlic, choose impeccably fresh, firm heads of garlic with no green sprouts. Separate the heads into cloves and peel them. Place the peeled cloves in a small heavy pot or frying pan and cover with the oil. Place on the stove over medium-low heat.

As soon as bubbles form around the garlic, turn the heat to low and cook the cloves until golden brown and completely soft. This will take anywhere from 20-40 minutes. Remove from the heat and cool. Covered and stored in the refrigerator, the garlic keeps for 1 month.

Spiced Pear, Beet and Red Onion Relish

Try this sweet and sour relish with Pepper and Garlic Cured Pork Chops, page 111, or with roast turkey.

Makes 3 cups (750 ml)

1 1/2 cups	water	375 ml
1/2 cup	sugar	125 ml
1/4 cup	red wine vinegar	60 ml
12	black peppercorns	12
4	whole cloves	4
4	1/4-inch (.5-cm) slices fresh ginger	4
1	medium beet, peeled and diced into 1/2-inch (1-cm) cubes	1
1 lb.	almost-ripe Bartlett pears, peeled, cored and diced into 1/2-inch (1-cm) cubes	450 g
1	medium red onion, peeled and thinly sliced into rings	1

Combine the water, sugar, vinegar, peppercorns, cloves, ginger and beets in a large pot. Bring to a boil and boil hard for 5 minutes. Add the pears and turn down to a simmer. Poach the pears until they are tender, 7-10 minutes. Remove from the heat and stir in the red onion. Cool to room temperature. The relish keeps for 3 weeks, covered and refrigerated.

Dried Fruit Mustard

We served this mustard with smoked black cod, but it can be used anywhere you would use Dijon mustard. Use any combination of dried fruit that suits your taste or pantry. Just make sure that the diced fruit totals 10 tablespoons (150 ml).

Makes 1 1/2 cups (375 ml)

1/2 cup	dry mustard	125 ml
1 cup	cold water	250 ml
2 tsp.	black mustard seeds	10 ml
	zest of one orange, finely chopped	
2 Tbsp.	diced apricots	30 ml
2 Tbsp.	diced crystallized ginger	30 ml
2 Tbsp.	diced dried figs	30 ml
2 Tbsp.	dried sour cherries or cranberries	30 ml
2 Tbsp.	golden raisins	30 ml
1/2 cup	white wine vinegar	125 ml
1/2 cup	sugar	125 ml
1 tsp.	salt	5 ml

Stir the dry mustard and water together until smooth. Heat a small, high-sided frying pan or pot over medium-high heat. Add the black mustard seeds and roast, shaking the pan constantly until the mustard seeds pop. Stir into the mustard mixture. Cover and let stand overnight.

The next day, place the orange zest and dried fruit in a bowl and cover with boiling water. Let stand for 5 minutes and drain.

Combine the vinegar, sugar and salt in a noncorrodible saucepan and bring to a boil. Turn the heat to medium and cook for 5 minutes. Add the mustard mixture and the fruit. Cook for 5 minutes, stirring constantly, until thickened and smooth. Remove from the heat and cool.

Taste the mustard and adjust it to taste with a bit more vinegar if you wish. Place the mustard in a sterilized jar, cover and refrigerate. The mustard keeps indefinitely if refrigerated.

Sweet and Sour Dipping Sauce

Try this sauce with spring rolls, sweet potato and prawn pancakes, crab fritters, chicken . . . and on and on. In fact, you will make up excuses just to use it!

Makes 3 cups (750 ml)

2 cups	granulated sugar	500 ml
1 1/2 cups	water	375 ml
4	cloves garlic, peeled and sliced	4
1/2	red pepper, green stem only removed	1/2
3 Tbsp.	fish sauce*	45 ml
5 Tbsp.	lemon juice	75 ml
1 tsp.	salt	5 ml
1 Tbsp.	hot chili paste,* or to taste	15 ml

*Available at Oriental markets and well-stocked supermarkets.

Place the sugar and water in a saucepan and bring to a boil. Boil for 10 minutes, remove from the heat and cool.

Place 1/2 cup (125 ml) of the sugar syrup and the remaining ingredients in the work bowl of a food processor or blender and blend until the pepper and garlic are puréed. The seeds will remain whole. Add the remaining sugar syrup and pulse briefly to combine. This sauce keeps almost forever, covered and refrigerated.

Chicken Stock

Makes about 2 quarts (2 L)

5 lbs.	chicken bones	2.2 kg
2	small onions, peeled and cut in half	2
1	medium carrot, peeled and cut in half	1
2	stalks celery, trimmed	2
1	head garlic, cut in half crosswise	1
1	bay leaf	1

Rinse the chicken bones and drain. Place them in a large stock pot and cover with 6 inches (15 cm) of cold water. Bring to a boil and skim off any foam that rises to the surface. Reduce the heat to a bare simmer and cook for half an hour, skimming the surface frequently.

Add the remaining ingredients and simmer for 6 hours, skimming off the fat and adding water as necessary. Strain the stock and cool. Cover and refrigerate. The next day, remove any fat that has congealed on the surface. The stock keeps for 4 days. For longer storage, freeze.

Beef or Veal Stock

Makes about 2 quarts (2 L)

5 lbs.	meaty beef or veal bones	2.2 kg
2	medium onions, peeled and cut into 1-inch (2.5-cm) pieces	2
1	large carrot, peeled and cut into 1-inch (2.5-cm) pieces	1
2	stalks celery, trimmed and cut into 1-inch (2.5-cm) pieces	2
2 Tbsp.	tomato paste	30 ml
1	bay leaf	1
10	whole black peppercorns	10

Preheat the oven to 400°F (200°C). Place the bones and vegetables in a single layer in one or two large roasting pans. Roast, turning the bones and vegetables occasionally, until lightly browned, about 30 minutes.

Smear the bones with the tomato paste and roast until dark brown, about 20-30 minutes. Scrape the bones and vegetables into a large stock pot. Pour 2 cups (500 ml) of water into the roasting pan and return to the oven for 15 minutes. Add the water to the stock pot, scraping to loosen the browned flavorful bits clinging to the pan.

Cover the bones with 6 inches (15 cm) of cold water and bring to a boil. Skim off any foam that rises to the surface. Reduce the heat to a bare simmer and cook for half an hour, skimming the surface frequently. Add the remaining ingredients and simmer for 8 hours, skimming off the fat and replenishing the water level as necessary. Strain the stock and cool. Cover and refrigerate. The next day, remove any fat that has congealed on the surface. The stock keeps for 4 days. Freeze for longer storage.

Beef or Veal Demi-Glace

Makes about 1 cup (250 ml)

Make Beef or Veal Stock, page 199, adding 1 cup (250 ml) of red wine along with the water.

The next day, after removing any congealed fat, place the stock in a large pot and bring to a boil. Continue boiling until the stock is reduced by three-quarters. Transfer to a smaller pot and cook on medium heat until reduced to 1 cup (250 ml).

Pour into a bowl and cool. Refrigerate overnight. Cut the demi-glace into 1-inch (2.5-cm) cubes, place in a plastic bag and freeze.

Index

About the Author

Award-winning chef Karen Barnaby started her cooking career in 1979 in Ottawa, Ontario, on a pink four-burner stove in the basement of the Bohemian Restaurant. She then moved on to the Rivoli restaurant and later the David Wood Food Shop in Toronto. At that time, she also taught at Dufflet's Great Cooks Cooking School. She decided to move west to Vancouver, British Columbia, where she worked at Capers before becoming the chef at the Raintree Restaurant. In 1992 she opened the Harvest Moon Cafe in Victoria and in 1994 the North 49 Restaurant and Market, and Restaurant Starfish in Vancouver.

Pacific Northwest magazine named her one of the region's best chefs in 1994. She is currently the executive chef at The Fish House in Stanley Park. The co-author of two books, the *David Wood Food Book* and the *David Wood Dessert Book,* Karen lives in Vancouver with her husband Steven McKinley, who is also a chef.